Interpersonal Strategies for System Management: Applications of Counseling and Participative Principles

Behavioral Science in Industry Series

Edited by Victor H. Vroom
Yale University

☐ COMMUNICATION PROCESSES IN ORGANIZATIONS
Lyman W. Porter, University of California, Irvine
Karlene H. Roberts, University of California, Berkeley

☐ FOUNDATIONS OF BEHAVIORAL SCIENCE RESEARCH IN ORGA-
NIZATIONS
*Sheldon Zedeck and Milton R. Blood, University of California, Ber-
keley*

☐ INTERPERSONAL STRATEGIES FOR SYSTEM MANAGEMENT: APPLI-
CATIONS OF COUNSELING AND PARTICIPATIVE PRINCIPLES
Raymond G. Hunt, Cornell University

MAN-MACHINE ENGINEERING
Alphonse Chapanis, The Johns Hopkins University

☐ MANAGEMENT OF COMPENSATION
Stephen J. Carroll and Allan N. Nash, University of Maryland

☐ MOTIVATION IN WORK ORGANIZATIONS
Edward E. Lawler III, The University of Michigan

OCCUPATIONAL PSYCHOLOGY
Donald E. Super, Teachers College, Columbia University
Martin J. Bohn, Jr.

ORGANIZATIONAL ANALYSIS: A SOCIOLOGICAL VIEW
Charles B. Perrow, State University of New York at Stony Brook

PERSONNEL SELECTION AND PLACEMENT
Marvin D. Dunnette, University of Minnesota

PSYCHOLOGY OF UNION-MANAGEMENT RELATIONS
Ross Stagner and Hjalmar Rosen, Wayne State University

SOCIAL PSYCHOLOGY OF THE WORK ORGANIZATION
Arnold S. Tannenbaum, The University of Michigan

TRAINING IN INDUSTRY: THE MANAGEMENT OF LEARNING
Bernard M. Bass, The University of Rochester
James A. Vaughan

☐ TRAINING: PROGRAM DEVELOPMENT AND EVALUATION
Irwin L. Goldstein, University of Maryland

☐ = II

Interpersonal Strategies for System Management: Applications of Counseling and Participative Principles

Raymond G. Hunt
Cornell University

Brooks/Cole Publishing Company
Monterey, California
A Division of Wadsworth Publishing Company, Inc.

TO KAREN

A map of the world that does not include
Utopia is not worth even glancing at, for it
leaves out the one country at which
Humanity is always landing. And when
Humanity lands there, it looks out and,
seeing a better country, sets sail. Progress is
the realization of Utopias.

Oscar Wilde
The Soul of Man Under Socialism, 1895

ISBN: 0-8185-0099-9
L.C. Catalog Card No.: 73-85594
Printed in the United States of America
1 2 3 4 5 6 7 8 9 10—78 77 76 75 74

Production Editor: Ginny Decker
Interior & Cover Design: Linda Marcetti
Illustration: John Foster
Typesetting: Continental Data Graphics, Culver City,
            California
Printing & Binding: Malloy Lithographing, Inc.,
            Ann Arbor, Michigan

preface

This book is for managers, counselors, and students of management and counseling. It is about work, people, organizations, policies, and the attitudes and beliefs necessary for effective management. My purpose is to show how democratic and humanistic values and dispositions may be actualized to enhance the quality of organizational life. The book can be used in a standard management or industrial psychology course. It can be a valuable supplementary source in courses concerned with the application of counseling concepts in community settings, and, of course, it can serve as a general reference work for practicing managers and for community mental-health workers. It can also be used as a text for university-, industry-, or government-sponsored workshop programs dealing either with interpersonal aspects of management or specifically with counseling.

I chose counseling and participative methods as instruments for achieving my objective in this book because (1) they fit democratic and humanistic specifications for managerial practice, (2) they themselves express the ethical principles undergirding those specifications, (3) they can easily be used by organizational leaders on a day-to-day basis, and (4) they are explicitly oriented to the basic interpersonal dimensions of organization but can be readily integrated with the structural and policy dimensions of organization. This last point is crucial: far too much of the management literature consists of over-simplified one-sided recommendations for sure-fire techniques to guarantee successful administration. Sometimes these recommendations stress personalities and human relations; sometimes they stress technical and mechanical devices such as automatic data processing, standardized personnel-selection methods, or one or another structural formula. Commonly, if they do the one, they leave no room for the other. This book undertakes to focus on interpersonal relations in order to show how organizational outcomes depend on the interaction of human personalities, social structures, and the environment surrounding the organization. It places the individual human being at the center of attention and stresses the idea that organizational processes are manifest in interpersonal transactions; at the same time, however, it emphasizes the idea that those processes

v

have other important determinants in addition to individual personalities.

It has been suggested that renewed interest in counseling and democratic management has come about in part because of concerns growing out of circumstances in some very different kinds of contemporary organizational environments (for instance, dehumanizing influences in vast bureaucracies on the one hand and increased opportunities for interpersonal friction in organic project-type organizations on the other). However that may be, I do not view counseling and participative management as panaceas for every dehumanizing organizational excrescence. They can help, yes, and the value premises from which they stem are essential to recognizing dehumanization when it happens. But policies and structures are also pertinent to the treatment and prevention of organizational dehumanization. Nor do I look on counseling and participation as devices for eliminating friction or conflict. People and their interests vary; as they figuratively rub against each other in organizations, sparks inevitably result. Counseling and participative practices provide ways to detect the smoldering fires that ensue, to keep them below organizational flashpoints, to adjudicate differences, to negotiate terms of association, and to use conflict constructively. Friction will not and indeed should not be eliminated; counseling simply provides ways of managing friction. If it were otherwise, work organizations would be dull places indeed, because interest germinates mostly from challenge, not from well-greased, robot-like programmed performances.

Books have histories and accrued indebtednesses as well as reasons for being written. In the case of this book, impetus and opportunity to work through the problems and issues associated with supervisory counseling and democratic management came in the Buffalo District Counseling Project, supported by the Internal Revenue Service. What made that project special were the uncommonly close and facilitative working relations it spawned. To the late John E. Foley, Buffalo District Director, a clear-headed, critical administrator, this book owes a very great deal. His interest, support, and challenge helped transform a research-and-development exercise into an intellectual adventure. And Donald Pellow, the District's Training Officer, is owed a substantial debt of gratitude not only for his ideas and help but even more for his patience and tolerance.

My colleague during the Buffalo District Counseling Project (and since), Cary M. Lichtman of Wayne State University, naturally contributed heavily to whatever merit this book may have. His help ranged from damping bad ideas to offering good ones; in addition, he drafted parts of materials adapted for use here in Chapters 2 and 7.

I would like to acknowledge the help of Victor H. Vroom, Yale University, editor of Brooks/Cole's Behavioral Science in Industry Series. Also, I would like to thank the reviewers of the manuscript for their helpful comments: Irwin A. Berg, Louisiana State University; G. A. Forehand, Educational Testing Service; Edward J. Morrison, University of Colorado; and, especially, C. Gilbert Wrenn, Macalester College.

Many other individuals and organizations gave something to this book, but they are so numerous and their roles were so varied that I could not name them all. There are a few, however, whom I must mention because they got so involved: Elizabeth Kemp, Peggy Leous, Dottie Stricker, and Betty Koehler. And I need to thank Bill Hicks and Ginny Decker of Brooks/Cole, who waited a long time yet remained consistently friendly, helpful, and supportive. Finally, I appreciate my wife Viola's support and forbearance (although she probably preferred me in the study rather than underfoot).

Raymond G. Hunt

contents

Introduction

Since modern organizations are not exempt from social realities, the discovery of creative ways of responding to persistent social pressures is a constant managerial challenge. This challenge has been heightened by an increasing demand for review of societal priorities, for revision of traditional bases and prerogatives of authority, for increased respect for the shared environment, for institutional renovation, for a wider sharing of power, and for a fairer allocation of society's resources. Change is as much a fundamental fact of life in the world of work as it is elsewhere in society, possibly more so. Few other spheres of social life confront so immediately or with such vital effect the contemporary coalescence of technical and human problems, and few require so constant and detailed an orientation toward the management of change. A lively sense of social responsibility and interpersonal sensitivity are therefore cornerstones of quality in management structures. The modern manager and supervisor of employees, whatever he manages and whomever he supervises, must understand the shifting nature of the contemporary organization, its environment, and the needs of its members. Today's manager must acquire sophistication about his organization's and his employees' preferred directions of development so that he may humanely and successfully accommodate his methods to the exigencies of a viscous social and technical order.

Models for Management

Neither nostalgia nor occasional contemporary exceptions should be allowed to cloud the realization that the model manager of 50 years ago is as out of place in today's environment as Attila the Hun at a peace rally. Prototypic military models that emphasize single-minded devotion to duty, preoccupation with power differentials, and coercion of conformity, along with rigid maintenance of bureaucratically prearranged, tradition-bound, hierarchic structures and procedures, may have a kind of romantic, "he-man" appeal in the lives of the Bengal Lancers, but they simply do not fit present-day realities. (Even the military is gradually making this painful discovery.)

The tough-minded, task-centered, no-nonsense entrepreneur of legend was at best adapted to a previous time and a special combination of organizational needs. Indeed, whether the prototypic hard-nosed captain of industry succeeded because of his approach or in spite of it is an intriguing question. Unfortunately, no one has an unambiguous answer. The point is that times and needs (or our understanding of them) have changed, and the tasks and requirements of management have changed with them. Consequently, a willingness to adapt concepts and methods to altered circumstances is an essential executive attribute.

Faced with the task of survival in a fluid environment, modern organizations are being forced to take stock of their customary modes of operation, organizational forms, and precepts of management. The inescapable conclusion usually has been that traditional bureaucratic concepts of management and kindred models for the organization of work (even if they were suited to an earlier, simpler, and more stable "sociotechnical" context) no longer serve the requirements of the present. New ideas about the structure, operation, and administration of work organizations have been required as bases for the development of organizational systems capable of harmonizing diverse pressures for performance in a constantly changing environment.

Nor does managerial challenge end with problems of administering technological change and insuring organizational adaptability. The human dimensions of organization and management have also grown more salient and over the long run must certainly overshadow the "hardware" dimensions, however difficult and complex the latter may be. In fact, technological and human problems of organization cannot be easily separated. Early glimpses of life in a computerized society already suggest that conclusion. Concepts of organization and management capable of integrating performance or task requirements and human needs into agreeable and productive operational systems plainly are required. But if it is imperative that we come to terms with human dimensions of work and organization, it is unfortunately also difficult. The needs and interests of people, individually and collectively, are variable and complex. What is more, they interconnect with forces and factors beyond the boundaries and narrow task responsibilities of particular work organizations. Understanding them requires paying attention to a diversity of factors: the characteristics of the work force (such as its size, distribution, educational and motivational levels), the presence or absence of alternative channels for expressing productive energy (for example, work versus play), cultural priorities (relating to beliefs about the nature and functions of work) and social responsibilities, and finally, individual differences—all these are germane to comprehension of the realities of organizational life.

The human resources with which modern organizations work are in many ways different and more diverse from what they were a generation ago. The average employee today is better educated than was his father. He is less passively disposed toward having his fate decided by others, however benevolent of attitude and intention those others may be. Today the worker seeks to find in a job means to ends other than mere survival. More often now he seeks avenues for self-expression and personal development. Most importantly, he wants to be treated as an individual, not as a "cog in a machine." Indeed, he (and she, ever more insistently now) demands such respect quite reasonably as a precondition of his own commitment to the enterprise.

Not only have workers changed as individuals; the social-cultural framework within which the work organization operates has also evolved. For a business to justify itself solely in terms of its profitability, efficiency, or number of jobs is no longer sufficient (if, indeed, it ever was). Nowadays it must articulate its relationship to wider social objectives and establish its legitimacy in terms of its contributions to the public welfare. In conclusion, the work organization in the "affluent society" has basic social as well as economic-technical responsibilities, and it must understand them well, even if it chooses to argue about them—perhaps especially if it wishes to argue about them. To remain viable, work organizations must endeavor to establish their relevance to the concerns of a modern world and demonstrate a readiness to contribute to achievement of the hopes and aspirations of the society of which they are part.

Organization and Management

In a certain sense, organizations are substitutes for the direct expression of individual human skill. By specialization and coordination they undertake to compensate for inevitable limitations on the capacities of particular human beings to satisfy the numerous requirements of productive enterprise. Thus, in the organization, collective action replaces exclusively individual action. Individual actions remain vital, but the *sine qua non* of organization is the orchestration of individual performances into a purposeful program resulting in a coherent effect—a determinate, more or less predictable, outcome. In short, the *sine qua non* of organization is found in performance of those coordinative and leadership functions commonly associated with the term *management*.

Strictly speaking, management is involved in all human conduct (as will become clear in Chapter 2); but in "simple" individual behavior, its role is ordinarily implicit. The management process is more prominent in the organizational setting where attempts are made to identify explicitly those integrative functions necessary to operation and to somehow allocate responsibility for their performance. The vast growth and proliferation of organizations in our modern era—what Kenneth Boulding called "The Organizational Revolution" (1968)—has heightened the importance of effective organizational leadership and management.

Since, as Boulding concisely put it, "an organization consists essentially of a bundle of roles tied together with communication" (p. 80), it must be apparent that getting information and knowing how to use it are critical organizational processes. Indeed Boulding has spoken of the "pathology of organizations," meaning failures of communication and information flow or inept use of the information that does flow. The problems are how to assure a satisfactory two-way, up-and-down flow of information and how to convert information into productive operating programs. Boulding graphically describes the main impediment to solution of these problems as the "corruption of information by hierarchy." The elaborately layered, structurally frozen, operationally ossified organization, with its status-based rules of association, makes communication at best problematical. As a result, a whole special profession of "organization doctors" (the felicitous phrase is Boulding's) has emerged dedicated to combating this organizational epidemic.

This book is concerned with these issues of information getting and communication. It is written from a perspective on enterprise management (more completely described in Chapters 2 and 4) that tries to keep in mind the complexity of organization, the reality of organizational structures, and the pertinence of various technologies to organizational affairs. At the same time, the book directs special attention to the human social dimensions of organizational behavior. Direct or indirect interchange (communication) among organizational members is the lifeblood of the organization, and human motivation, joined with plans for its expression, is the engine that pumps it.

The interpersonal competency of management is a crucial *technical* variable in organizational performance. Possession of sophisticated interpersonal strategies is an essential managerial prerequisite. However, people stand at the center of the organizational stage for an even more important reason: organizations should be worked not only by but *for* human beings. Sound management cannot be grounded on strictly technical foundations; it can be based only in humanistic premises and defined only against ultimate criteria of social welfare.

Hence this book is about management, but it is also about morality. Confrontation with ethical issues is indispensable to stating a complete view of the functions and requirements of management. If, as Boulding suggests (and I agree), a moralist should also be a social scientist—alive to the bodies of knowledge relevant to his ethical judgments—it is nonetheless true organizationally and therefore managerially that the "basic question is by what standards do we appraise institutions, policies, or even people; what constitutes 'betterment' or 'worsening'?" (Boulding, 1968, p. xiv).

As you will see, I have made some rather firm decisions about these matters. They are stated most systematically in Chapter 2, but I have expressly tried to identify the ethical assumptions and implications of positions taken and prescriptions offered throughout the book. If I were to summarize the moral-ethical attitudes you could expect to encounter in the pages of this book, three words probably would do it: humanism, participation, democracy.

It is hard not to be bothered and puzzled by why it should be true that, as Irving Bluestone (1972) of the United Auto Workers has pointedly observed, "the work place is probably the most authoritarian environment in which the adult finds himself. Its rigidity and denial of freedom lead people to live a kind of double life: at home they enjoy substantially the autonomy and self-fulfillment of free citizens; at work they are subject to constant regimentation, supervision and control by others."

Regimentation, supervision, and control mostly rest on prerogatives of status. They are justified by invoking needs for efficiency and production requirements. By itself efficiency is simply a sensible organizational aspiration; it becomes a bone of contention only when it is transformed into a managerial fetish that is subject solely to "technical" criteria. It is certainly true that an organization can stay alive only if it *produces*. Productivity is an integral component of organizational "health." But the organization is not a machine. Production, in the final analysis, depends heavily on human motivation, on cooperation, on willingness, on consent. And these, at base, are voluntary matters. In the following vivid statement, Bluestone draws out the issues latent in this proposition:

> In a democracy, the rules of society are fashioned with the consent of those who must live by them . . . In the work place, management decides the rules to be lived by and arbitrarily imposes its will by exercising its authority to impose disciplinary sanctions in case of individual transgression.
>
> The argument in support of the authoritarianism of the work place is that the organization of production and the goal of maximizing profit make it mandatory. Ownership means control. Ownership means rule by decree. Thus, the pattern of relations between the "governors" and the "governed" in the business enterprise is diametrically contradictory to the democratic way of life.
>
> This contradiction lies at the heart of the problems with which labor-management relations must grapple . . .*

Bluestone's references are to business organizations and are heavily conditioned by his experiences in the industrial sector. However,

---

*I. Bluestone, "Democratizing the Work Place." Detroit, United Automobile Workers, Mimeo, June 22, 1972. Reprinted by permission of the author.

to generalize and assume that things are greatly different in other species of work organization would be a major mistake; they aren't. Bluestone sounds a warning as cogent to nonbusiness managers as it is to those in business organizations:

> New directions are stirring as new problems arise. Cracks are occurring in the traditional discipline of the work place. Absenteeism has been tending upward. The "Monday" and "Friday" absentee is more commonplace. Tardiness shows an upward trend. Labor turnover increases. The boredom and repetitiveness of jobs are accompanied by "job alienation" and departure from the "work ethic," in turn resulting in a deterioration of attention to production and quality. Workers feel a loss of individuality, dignity, self-respect. They lose a sense of job satisfaction. And they question the current ways of doing things as they seek to change the inflexible restrictions put upon them by the production process.

What Bluestone calls for in blunt terms is bringing the "democratic institution of society into the work place"—not literally, of course, but spiritually, philosophically. What exactly democracy is in practice admittedly is not all that obvious, but luckily that is not the nub of the matter. In *Management and Machiavelli* (1967), Antony Jay's provocative and widely read (often for the wrong reasons) book, the thesis is advanced that democracy is basically "an attitude, an instinct, a way of doing things, which consults people in advance and takes account of their views, wishes, and ideas before making final decisions" (p. 223). I would take Jay's conception a bit further to cover methods of implementing as well as making decisions, but the important point is that democracy is not a particular form or structure. It is a process, a basic way of operating. Its hallmark obviously is *participation*.

A democratic organization is one that operates democratically. It will be characterized by a widespread sharing of power and participatory processes at all levels. And it will justify its forms and methods not in terms of "pressure from the union" or some other equally specious external force but by reference to central humanistic values.

Resistance to these precepts on grounds that they lead to erosion of traditional privilege is understandable; opposition to them on organizational grounds is not, especially as organizations become larger and more complicated. In the first place, while organizations are many things, prominent among those things is their status as *political* institutions. They are populated with interest groupings having specialized functions and control over selected kinds of information (more about that later). As a result, there is a structural need for multiple centers of effective counterbalancing power in order for an organization to work at all well. Alfred Sloan saw this clearly and organized his administration of the General Motors Corporation around its implications. I suggest that information-seeking and decentralization of decision processes, by simple extension, imply more employee participation.

Also related to the political issue of intraorganizational interest groupings is the problem of motivating or mobilizing the resources of an organization around common objectives. Success in doing this plainly involves negotiation and adjudication of competing interests. Except perhaps in the very short run, compulsion is useless. "Once you accept that large organizations usually triumph over small ones, you accept that 'managed' industries will succeed 'bossed' ones" (Jay, 1967, p. 2).

Finally, there is a peculiarly pernicious yet common misunderstanding about what management is. It is manifest in the fallacious equating of management with managers, but, in fact, management is a *function*. It can be (and, in reality, is) performed by anybody or everybody in an organization, subject really only to criteria of competence. "Manager," on the other hand, is an *office*, a position. It is a role differentiated for organizational convenience and allocated special responsibilities for performance of acknowledged management functions. As a role it is arbitrary and so neither equivalent to management nor sacred. In the secular organization there is no inherent reason (although there may be practical ones) why management functions cannot be variously distributed throughout an organization; indeed, they always are in practice, as the concept of the "informal" organization attests. Hence, participatory management, in a technical sense, is no more than a redistribution of organizational responsibilities to satisfy management requirements. In other words, participatory management is a redefinition of management roles that can actually be a matter of common organizational interest. In this book, Chapter 4 illustrates a way of applying the participative democratic attitude to a modest restructuring of organizational roles—modest in that it does little to alter the nondemocratic trappings of the system, although it is intended to impact modes of operating and making policies.

Human Relations and "Human Relations"

"Human relations" are featured in this book, and therein lies an intellectual risk. The risk is that my viewpoint will be confused with the so-called Human Relations school of organizational-managerial thought. That would be unfortunate because, despite good intentions, the Human Relations tradition, like Potiphar's wife, has acquired something of a bad name.

Theoretical difficulties with the Human Relations orientation, as I have remarked in greater detail elsewhere (see Lichtman & Hunt, 1971), have to do chiefly with its errors of omission and not so much with any of commission. Because of its preoccupation with the "informal" organization and worker personalities, Human Relations theorizing never achieved a fully realized, balanced understanding of organization. It badly neglected the technology-structure-policy nexus of organization that I talk more about in later chapters, especially Chapter 2.

The Human Relations school earned its dubious reputation for another reason, too. As applied in the work setting, it leads to a variety of managerial gimmicks and manipulative practices rationalized as beneficial to workers but too often constituting counterfeit currency. Once more Irving Bluestone has an incisive observation: "Creating a pleasant, decent management team is desirable, but it does not alter the basic managerial authoritarian design. 'Human engineering' [or Human Relations] concepts may appear to establish more comfortable employer-employee relations, but they are primarily manipulative of the workers; managerial administration remains fundamentally unchanged." On this subject of "manipulation," you will find the Bennis-Gomberg-Marrow exchange about the "true" character of certain "classic" human relations experiments, published a few years ago in the periodical *Trans-action* (Vol. 2, 1965) interesting and informative reading. Among other things, the assertions and counterassertions stated there depict how radically different things can appear when they are viewed from different vantage points.

At any rate, the matter of manipulation of the worker warrants further special commentary here because of some of the procedural ideas I broach in later chapters. Specifically, in Chapter 8 I present discussions of behavior-modification techniques and review the concept of "behavioral engineering." Much more could be said than I shall say here, but really the fundamental question that needs to be answered is straightforward: just what is it that makes a practice "manipulative"? I have already suggested the answer: whether a practice is or is not manipulative turns on the degree of democratization existing in the setting of its use.

In his engaging book *Managerial Psychology* (1964), Harold Leavitt relates several alternative "change models" that can help elaborate and clarify this answer. Leavitt describes what he calls "authoritarian, manipulative, and collaborative" models. The authoritarian model is familiar already. The more interesting and difficult distinctions are in the manipulative and collaborative models.

Leavitt characterizes *manipulation* as a way of solving the problem of "getting somebody to do something you want without using authority" (p. 183). As a solution, manipulation rests on five key ideas:

1. That *A*'s (the changer's) motives are not known to *B* (the changee).
2. That the relationship between *A* and *B* is used as a tool for influence (that is, the relationship is used exploitatively).
3. That there is also exploitation of *B*'s dependency on *A*.
4. That *A* displays considerable sophistication about the psychology of the individual (that is, the changer plays on *B*'s needs and feelings).
5. That the hallmark of manipulative change is gradualness—one cannot manipulate successfully with a hoop and a holler.

Thus manipulation is a two-step process: first build an interpersonal relationship, then use it, carefully and disingenuously. If it can be dressed up to look like participative decision-making, so much the better (or worse).

Collaborative change strategies, on the other hand, also stress relationships between *A* and *B* and their roles as instruments for change, but within the philosophical and operational framework we have labeled as "democratic." And, like manipulative strategies, collaborative ones emphasize attention to individual needs and interests. The difference is that collaboration is founded on the humanistic value of respect for the individual instead of on the crassly pragmatic value of expediency. A collaborative change is help-oriented and leaves the worker in control of the process. Its essentials as a solution to the problem of change are as follows:

1. *B* perceives the existence of a problem, a need for change (he may be helped in this by his supervisor, *A*).

2. B takes responsibility for seeking alternatives to the present state of affairs (again A can help).
3. A and B mutually communicate about the implications of the various alternatives identified.
4. B selects some alternative A can accept. A commits to a criterion of "acceptable" rather than one of "ideal" (that is, what is ideal or acceptable from A's point of view. A's "acceptable" could be B's "ideal," and that of course would be the millennium).
5. B tries to change and A supports the effort (and may himself have to change along the way).
6. B, with A's help, tries to develop new patterns of performance.

Leavitt draws a parallel between this collaborative-change model and the practice of nondirective counseling, which I discuss in Chapter 8. He also draws a less convincing analogy to the methods of Alcoholics Anonymous.* But whatever exemplification is used, it must be obvious that quite a thin line separates collaboration from manipulation; where the one begins and the other ends can sometimes prove a challenging task of discovery. Furthermore, it is important not to allow the scare-word "manipulation" to become a barrier to experimenting with and implementing motivational and participative managerial strategies. One needs to beware straw men almost as much as demogogues, even though comfort can be taken from the fact that each will be exposed in the end.

Manipulation and Motivation

In the following pages I describe a problem-focused, employee-centered, motivational approach to management. It represents an application to the management process of a view of organizations as complex social systems. Its great guiding principle (if it has one) is that a manager's primary task is the management of relations—in systems jargon, "interfaces." These relations, especially the interpersonal ones, are the eternal verities of organizational life.

The ways by which relations may be managed are many. Mainly, however, the general idea is to arrange conditions in the relationship

*Less convincing because the indications are that AA works from the requirement that B, the changee, renounce any belief that he is the master of his fate (so far as alcohol is concerned anyway), a philosophy for living with which I cannot get comfortable.

and its environment such that the parties to it are *motivated* to organize their actions around a mutually acceptable set of terms and objectives. I would emphasize again (and will keep on emphasizing) the requirements for reciprocity in this process at the same time that I allocate responsibility for leadership in guaranteeing its accomplishment to the manager. I wish to give the manager some genuine right to a sense of moral rectitude.

I have neither the space nor the inclination to enter here a technical discourse on matters motivational. You should be forewarned, however, that I shall be using terms such as "motivate" and even "to motivate" somewhat freely and, strictly speaking, loosely. What I wish consistently to mean, though, is a process centered in the basic supervisory relationship that is attentive to human needs and that is conducted after the democratic-collaborative fashion. This process will, one way or another, affect the "inner" motives of the persons involved, mainly by causing greater levels of satisfaction, although other possibilities cannot be excluded. In operation, motivational strategies will resemble the kinds of events and procedures psychologists now talk about under the heading "incentive motivation." In job settings, this comes to working with the *conditions* of work so as to enhance the benefits and decrease the costs associated with job performance.

Frequently this will be facilitated, even made possible, by rearranging the organization's structure (its design, chain of command, work-flow systems, and what not) or by altering its general operating policies (such things as compensation programs). Routinely and daily, however, the organization operates in and through a network of interpersonal relations. It is in that face-to-face environment that the organization's nature is made real to its members (and its observers), and it is unwise to leave the management of that environment to chance. The manager needs a pole star to orient his course; for that function I commend the counseling concept.

The modern enterprise, I have maintained, is caught up in a perplexing search for means to improve effectiveness of its performance in an uncertain environment while at the same time reconciling its operations with the insistent human and social requirements of the world. How to individualize, humanize, and democratize organizations while enhancing their productivity is thus a broad, basic question to which answers must be found. The concept of counseling outlined in this book, I believe, can help in that quest.

Counseling and Management

By "counseling" I basically mean modes by which a supervisor can go about building and sustaining vital working relationships with individual subordinates—relations that are consistent with and facilitate the maintenance of both high performance standards and satisfying human relations. In other words, I regard counseling essentially as an *approach* to management targeted to the critical human interfaces. As such, it is neither an end in itself nor simply a specific set of formal skills or techniques. Skill is involved, to be sure, but counseling like democracy is more essentially "a state of mind," a complex of goals and principles guiding supervisory performance.

In the book *Revolution in Counseling* (1966), Joseph Shoben gives voice to some feelings of disquiet that I share about the potential for dehumanization implicit in a preoccupation with "methods." It is essential, he insists, that methods be understood as means to ends. Certainly they warrant review and analysis on their merits, but they must not divert attention from reflection on and careful specification of the ends to which the means are addressed, nor from the value system that rationalizes and justifies the whole means-end scheme. Critical attention to ends, values, and the central dignity of the individual are pre-eminent points of reference. Methods are important—obviously we couldn't do without them—but they are nevertheless secondary. In Chapter 2, I describe two distinct modes of organizational system analysis, and in Chapters 4 and 8 I discuss the general question of goal-setting.

The counseling state of mind expresses a particular philosophy of management. It represents a coalescence in the immediate superior-subordinate relationship of basic social-technical trends in Western industrial societies, a coalescence capable of harmonizing the task and human functions of supervision.

Because I view the concept of counseling mainly as a means of expressing a particular managerial ethic, appreciation of that ethic is an obvious necessity. Accordingly, Chapter 3 is devoted to discussion of the managerial-supervisory role. I review the functions of work supervisors and examine some of the ways these functions may be implemented, giving special emphasis to the effects of differing approaches to the supervisory task. In the process I endeavor to sketch a philosophy of supervision and management into which counseling functions can fit as workable means to supervisory ends.

I have repeatedly stated that the most congenial basic managerial philosophy is essentially humanistic, democratic, and "person-centered." At the same time it is a philosophy that assumes no inherent categorical incompatibility between performing a task and being happy. Doing a job and being happy in the process sometimes is difficult and, under some conditions, even impossible. Nevertheless, I believe that a fundamental managerial responsibility involves searching for ways of *simultaneously* maximizing (or at least improving) the effectiveness of organizations, both in the performance of tasks and in meeting the needs of people. Utopian as it may sound, achievement of this social goal is the ultimate measure of an organization's quality.

Thus it is in the interest of organizations to cultivate employee-centered dispositions in their supervisors via training and orientation programs as well as by usual selection procedures. But, to ensure that these newer perspectives eventuate in improved performance, the supervisor must be provided with instrumental skills necessary to the implementation of employee-centered objectives. Some of these skills repose in knowledge of the workings of organizations and the human beings who populate them; the spreading practice of introducing heavy doses of behavioral science into management-training programs is an important recognition of this fact. However, if the supervisor is to deal effectively with the interpersonal unit, he needs an array of technical interpersonal skills rarely taught in either business schools or in-service training programs. Paramount among those interpersonal skills is the ability to establish and implement a productive counseling relation. As Rensis Likert observed in his highly influential book, *New Patterns of Management* (1961), "Any organization which bases its operation on [the newer theory] will necessarily make use of individual counseling and coaching by superiors of subordinates."

Both individual and group counseling methods, which I outline in later chapters, will be useful to the modern manager. However, he will need to be skilled in deciding what situations call for which procedures as well as capable of using both separately. Furthermore, a manager needs to recognize that the range of problems to which supervisory counseling may be fruitfully applied is apt to extend beyond the narrow confines of the "job" to include subordinates' hopes, aspirations, frustrations, and the like. It is therefore crucial that supervisors learn where and how to draw the limits of legitimate problems so as to avoid the unwitting but consuming practice of implicit psychiatry.

I shall be at some pains to free the concept of counseling I present from any "clinical" connotations. I wish to make it plain that I am not talking about psychoanalysis, psychotherapy, or any similar process in this book. I plan to draw on the experience and wisdom of professional counselors and clinicians in human relations, but what concerns me exclusively are the ways supervisors and managers can go about achieving the goals of work organizations. For that reason I like to describe my concept of counseling as "problem-focused" and "task-oriented" as well as "person- or employee-centered." I shall try to make the distinction clear as I go along, but generally what I have in mind by a person-centered/problem-focused concept of counseling is this: while the needs and interests of the individual worker are primary starting points in managerial planning as well as criteria for organizational achievement, procedurally management's attention should fasten on task performance, behavior, and problem-solving rather than on the larger personality attributes of the worker. I harbor no aspirations of converting managers into practicing clinicians—far from it. By encouraging a broadened viewpoint and attention to employee needs and interests, I am hoping only to help managers and supervisors be better at their jobs. That in itself is a sufficiently demanding objective. My adapted ideas about the supervisory counseling of employees, therefore, are consistently and pointedly directed toward finding ways of relating to and working with people, not changing them.

Chapter 4 translates these concepts into organizationally feasible development programs. Some methods for initiating the development of counseling skills on the part of work supervisors are described in some detail, together with consideration of more general strategies for increasing organizational effectiveness. The particular procedures described are, obviously, not the only ones that might be used. Their presentation is intended to be mainly illustrative. In any case, that chapter (and Chapter 7 as well) is mainly concerned with training formats and follow-on support for instructional efforts.

Finally, in Chapters 8 and 9 is an exposition of some of the problems, impediments, practical dilemmas, and ethical confrontations my experience has indicated may be anticipated in the course of attempts to implement counseling concepts and/or person-centered styles of supervision. Chapter 8 includes, in addition, some consideration of extensions of the counseling concept to group methods of supervision and a brief survey of some alternative and special-purpose counseling or behavior-change procedures.

A Closing Comment on Rationality in Management

You will soon find that the model of management expressed here carries a staunchly rationalistic tone. Now we all know full well that actual organizational behavior is rarely rational; theories of management that suggest otherwise are more dream than reality. Yet, almost paradoxically, managerial behavior is consistently and justly subject to "norms of rationality." It is fair to expect that managers will *try* to be sane, to behave rationally (even when it isn't perfectly clear what that means). Organizational theorists especially (but practical managers, too) need to be realistic about the idiosyncrasies of organizational life. They must not allow their wishes (or models) to get confused with reality. So much is unquestionable. But at the same time one cannot found managerial philosophies or practices on theorems of caprice; managers need at least to try to bring order to recalcitrant systems and to strive to develop criteria that tell them when they have achieved it.

References

Bennis, W. Beyond bureaucracy. *Trans-action*, 1965, **2**, 31–35.

Bluestone, I. Democratizing the work place. Detroit, United Automobile Workers, 1972, mimeo.

Boulding, K. E. *The organizational revolution: A study of the ethics of economic organization.* Chicago: Quadrangle, 1968.

Gomberg, W. The trouble with democratic management. *Trans-action*, 1965, **2**, 30–31.

Gomberg, W. Harwood's "press agentry." *Trans-action*, 1965, **2**, 35–36.

Gomberg, W. Democratic management—Gomberg replies. *Trans-action*, 1966, **4**, 48.

Jay, A. *Management and Machiavelli: An inquiry into the politics of corporate life.* New York: Bantam, 1967.

Leavitt, H. J. *Managerial psychology.* (Rev. ed.) Chicago: University of Chicago Press, 1964.

Lichtman, C. M. & Hunt, R. G. Personality and organization theory. *Psychological Bulletin*, 1971, **76**, 271–294.

Likert, R. *New patterns of management.* New York: McGraw-Hill, 1961.

Marrow, A. Gomberg's "fantasy." *Trans-action*, 1965, **2**, 36–37, 56.

Shoben, E. J., Jr. Personal worth in education and counseling. In J. D. Krumboltz (Ed.), *Revolution in counseling*. Boston: Houghton Mifflin, 1966. Pp. 49–79.

Recommended Readings

Burby, R. J. *An introduction to the basic supervision of people*. Reading, Mass.: Addison-Wesley, 1966. (An elementary, but helpful, very practically disposed work.)

McGuire, J. W. *Business and society*. New York: McGraw-Hill, 1963. (A readable, thoughtful discourse on the role of business in modern society.)

Reich, C. A. *The greening of America*. New York: Random House, 1970. (The controversial representative of the "new" developing aspirations and requirements for organizations from a "radicalized society.")

Ruitenbeek, H. M. *The dilemma of organizational society*. New York: Dutton, 1963. (A handy anthology of writings on various aspects of the organizational scene.)

Schmidt, W. H. *Organizational frontiers and human values*. Belmont, Calif.: Wadsworth, 1970. (A variety of papers presenting "a preview of the critical social and physical changes anticipated in our environment and the impact they will have upon the goals, functions, structures, and relationship of our organizations.")

chapter
two

Effective Organizations: System Perspectives

A few pages back, I remarked on contemporary concerns for finding ways of improving the effectiveness of organizations. However, saying that a long-term objective of management should be the improvement of organizational performance comes to little more than mouthing slogans unless we provide a definition of relevant performance dimensions and criteria for their evaluation. Therefore, we need to become more specific about what organizational effectiveness is, and we must set out the essentials of theory that guide and support the judgments offered. As I said in Chapter 1, managers need knowledge and sophistication about the workings of organizations in order to perform well within organizations. Hence this chapter reviews the idea of effectiveness at some length and deals with questions about how to define and then encourage and evaluate organizational achievement. The bulk of the chapter is devoted to describing a way of looking at organizations and their component elements as social systems and using that perspective as a basis for developing a workable understanding of what organizational effectiveness means in practice as well as in theory.

As implied in Chapter 1, my ultimate intention is to place the idea of organizational effectiveness in a particular context of motivational strategies for accomplishing organizational goals and objectives. Eventually, I shall relate counseling to this concept of organizational effectiveness in two ways: (1) as a kind of integrating orientation and (2) as a tactical means of its operational realization. I can begin to lay a conceptual foundation for this concept by raising some detailed questions about organizational goal-setting and problem-solving and then going on to a more general analysis of related organizational processes.

Organizational Goals and Organizational Effectiveness

No one really doubts the general idea that, in some sense, all organizations can be said to have objectives or goals. But the problem of conceptualizing an organization's goals is complicated. Therefore, attempts at focusing on organizational goals and their achievement in order to define or measure effectiveness face real difficulties, and the practice has not lacked for critics. Some commentators point out how difficult it is to identify just what an organization's goals are—at least to do it well enough to permit their measurement. Others remark on the phenomenon of organizational complexity and raise the question of just whose goals will serve to define the organization's objectives. Think, for example, of some of the issues that prolong and intensify labor-management contract negotiations or the struggles between quality-conscious technical specialists and cost-conscious financial managers. In addition to these points of contention, a troubling subjectivity often enters into judgments about goal achievement. When questions about whether goals have been reached are settled according to somebody's emotional feelings, the chances for dispute clearly are plural.

Without necessarily denying the existence of goals in organizations, these difficulties have nevertheless prompted several theorists to reject goals as final criteria for deciding questions of organizational effectiveness and to favor some other alternative. Although I shall wish to qualify it later, one of these alternatives deserves special mention because it conveys a sagacious understanding of the basic properties of organizations.

In 1967, two behavioral scientists, Ephraim Yuchtman and Stanley E. Seashore, proposed what they call a system-resource approach to organizational effectiveness. Their thesis is that effectiveness is represented by an organization's continuing success in carrying out competitive transactions involving the scarce and valued internal and external resources necessary to its operations. At any moment in time an organization's effectiveness is equivalent to its "bargaining position"—that is, its ability to acquire and suitably deploy resources —in a given environment.

Resources, Maintenance, and Performance

Basic to this definition of bargaining position is the idea that every organization exists in an environment in which it competes with every other organization to obtain the resources necessary for survival. Some resources are more plentiful than others, and there are, of course, many different kinds of resources. However, all resources relate to one or both of an organization's two primary functional requirements: maintenance and performance (production). Organizational survival depends on the availability of the resources needed to meet both of these requirements.

Maintenance resources are those that sustain the system. In social systems such as organizations, this involves, in addition to various material resources, what Katz and Kahn (1966) describe as "holding the human parts in the system and mobilizing their energies in prescribed patterns" (p. 33). For the organization to continue its existence, persons must be motivated to "belong" to it and be able and willing to conform to its operating rules.

Strictly speaking, essential to organizational system maintenance are the attraction and retention of the skills and other capabilities necessary for its operation. People, as such, are not the required resources; what organizations need are things (such as talents and attitudes) that only people typically have and that cannot be disassociated from them as individuals. If you will imagine a totally and perfectly automated factory in a completely and permanently congenial environment, it will be evident that you are imagining an organizational system wherein maintenance resources ordinarily supplied by real individual persons are being self-generated by magic machines. The improbability of such a system outside of science fiction underscores the vital importance of people to the maintenance (and performance) of organizational systems. Leaving aside physical resources (machines, buildings, and so on, which are also maintenance resources), skills, aptitudes, and ideas come packaged as human resources. They are intermixed with a multitude of other human characteristics that combine to influence the *motivations* of individuals to make their capabilities available and to apply them within particular organizations. Thus by maintenance resources I mean the physical facilities, people (including their motivations), and associated supporting conditions necessary to continued existence and operation of an organization.

As distinguished from maintenance resources, performance or production resources are those processed to yield outputs. They include raw materials in the usual sense (iron, rubber, coal) and also the technology employed in the conversion of raw materials to output. Under certain circumstances, these resources may also be people, as they are in schools or prisons. When this is true, I speak of "people-processing" organizations and of "people-processing" technologies.

As in other things, organizations differ in the kind and quantity of resources they require. Labor-intensive service industries, for instance, will have quantitatively if not qualitatively different personnel-resource requirements from capital-intensive machine-tool industries. For example, an aerospace research-and-development laboratory will require a mix of skills quite different from those needed by a retail-clothing store.

Yet there are ways in which all organizations are in competition. Resources are in finite supply, needs for some overlap, and there is less-than-perfect substitutability of one resource for another. The research-and-development laboratory and the clothing outlet, for example, both require capital as well as space, personnel, financial management, and other common resources. Their ability to command these resources—to get them, keep them, and use them—is a comparative measure of their relative effectiveness. An organization is effective to the extent that it can survive and control its own fate.

It might seem to follow from this proposition that achievement of monopolistic status is the epitome of organizational effectiveness. And in a sense it is, provided that the monopoly is absolute in that the organization has complete control over all relevant resources. So imperial a status, however, is about as improbable as the fictional firm operating untouched by human hands. This is so because, in the first place, there are laws about such things as restraint of trade and the like. But even if there weren't, it is just too hard to be feasible for any organization to control absolutely any and all resources it now or conceivably in the future might require; moreover, even if it could control absolutely the material resources it needs, that very power would almost certainly erode badly the social good-will crucial to the survival of any organization. It is a universal fact of managerial life that some things have to be given up in order that other things can be secured. Whether they understood it that way or not, even the so-called Robber Barons (those self-seeking turn-of-the-century financier/speculators, renowned more for their exploitative pursuit of gold than for any gentler social impulses) discovered the need for making trades among maintenance and production resources (including requirements for returning benefits to society—the need to pay one's social rent, as it were). It is thus generally advisable in the real world to try optimizing rather than maximizing effectiveness; there simply are too many dimensions to organizations to maximize them all at once. Further, some of those dimensions are mutually contradictory; besides, it usually isn't even known what a "maximum" is.

Goals Again

The notion that I have been stating as a general definition of effectiveness—that is, organizational power over the resources necessary for operation—precludes any particular goal from consideration as an ultimate criterion for effectiveness. Realistically, the resources needed for organizational performance are many and diverse; moreover, they change in number and kind as circumstances change. Needs for venture capital, for instance, will depend on the nature and scope of opportunities. In addition, the competitive relationships pertinent to the acquisition and use of resources are multiple, and some if not all classes of resources are interchangeable. So no single organizational goal can be permanently pre-eminent (except possibly the very general one of survival). But no thoughtful person can conclude from these arguments that goals and goal-setting are irrelevant to organizational affairs. On the contrary, they are highly relevant. Indeed, they are fundamental to the ideas expressed throughout this book.

Yuchtman and Seashore (1967) observe that by stating particular goals the organization can define targets and guidelines for enhancing its bargaining position. Managerial injunctions to increase market share by 5% in the next fiscal year can help to energize and organize action while providing a criterion against which to evaluate performance. However, achievement of that objective at the cost of precipitating federal antitrust action or a thoroughly disgruntled sales department will leave moot any question of the entire organization's effectiveness. The organization's interests are not defined by a single goal, nor are they always defined by the original goals that may have been set. Decisions about an organization's effectiveness need to be broadly based. They need to take account of many goals and of side effects, too. Goals are also pertinent organizationally in the sense that they identify the aspirations and interests of individual members or of subgroups. Goals define what individuals and groups seek and hence what resources are needed to sustain the motivation to belong to and perform within the organization. One man wants satisfaction from a job well done; another only wants enough income to allow devoted pursuit of the pleasures of the flesh, with as little thought about his job as possible. Employees on the assembly line want an easier time of it; employees in the sales office want more and cheaper cars. In each case, what counts in the end is not the organization's success in achieving a particular goal but its overall capability as a resource-getting system regularly able to satisfy the many shifting requirements for its performance, including the varied goals of its individual members.

In practical terms, the process of enhancing organizational effectiveness will be characterized and measured by the *durable* achievement of discrete subgoals. These aggregate through time to describe something progressively different and, presumably, organizationally better. Goals need to be conceptualized as targets for the application of resources. Only in that way can it become clear exactly what resources are required. The idea of an effective organization then translates into an ability to get the resources to achieve the manifold of goals set for it. In a competitive environment (and all natural environments are competitive) this bargaining capability will depend on the organization's aggregate wisdom and skill as a resource-using system—that is, on the soundness of the operational strategies it selects (including goal-setting). Therefore, finding multidimensional criteria for and approaches to promoting and assessing organizational effectiveness is essential to successful management. To do this, the manager requires a suitable perspective on the general nature of organizations. Such a perspective should do justice to the complexity of organizations and at the same time afford conceptual tools for coping with that complexity. And, of course, it should supply a framework for intelligent resource management that can eventuate in more effective organizations.

Modern Organizational Theory and the Concept of System

In the preceding pages I have used the words "system" and "systems" in a casual way. Now the time has come to be more explicit about the meanings I wish these terms to convey, for the concept of the system is basic to so-called modern organizational theory. Conceiving of organizations as systems emphasizes their dynamic nature, the interdependency of their parts, the special significance of their continuing relations with surrounding environments, and their nature as social emergents. This last point is fundamental. It signifies the reality of organization. The character and functions of a system will be found not merely in the discrete elements of which it is constructed but in its design as well. The organization emerges from the patterns by which its parts are interrelated. Hence, as I suggested in Chapter 1, organizational design (or structure) will be among the major determinants of events within the system and of outputs from it. In other words, the same elements put together differently define different systems that produce different consequences.

For example, an organization providing technical support services (computer services) to various line organizations (engineering, production, marketing) could be structured in alternative ways without changing the cast of characters or the actual work being done. By a set of those policy decisions I alluded to earlier, one organization might establish cross-sections of its staff as subdepartments assigned to support individual line organizations. Or, following a different policy, another organization might maintain a pool of technical personnel for assignment to tasks as these are requested. Other alternatives may exist, but these two examples illustrate how organizational designs structure the critical relationships (or interfaces) within a system. Output variations associated with the second as compared with the first of the designs mentioned might be (1) greater efficiency in use of resources by the support organization through reduction of idling time, (2) problems in meeting tight schedules in line organizations because of lack of control over resources, (3) diminished job satisfaction on the part of pooled personnel, and (4) better-quality performance by the support organization because of an ability to use highly skilled personnel in operational capacities instead of diverting them to administrative functions. In any event, altering the pattern of relations that is the structure of an organization will carry with it variations of one kind or another in its outputs. As a corollary to this structural premise, I presume that organizations tend to preserve whatever structural form they have. This tendency toward stability may arise from a still more basic proclivity among systems (human systems anyway) to avoid uncertainty. In any case, it can be termed their *conservational dynamic.*.

Organizations are inclined to remain the same, to perpetuate the *status quo.* But they also tend to change, especially when they exist in an environment that itself is fluid in some degree. This organizational predilection toward change may be called the *transformational dynamic* of organizations. Balancing and managing the two processes of change and constancy must be a fundamental focus of organization administration. The frequent implicit collisions of these two processes represent an often unrecognized source of administrative dilemmas. Relating an organizational system to changing environmental events while simultaneously trying to preserve its institutional character is no simple trick. To be persuaded of the truth of these elementary thoughts, one need only reflect on the degree to which the American military has agonized over such questions as how far it can go in allowing the visible growth of hair on its members without impairing the image and integrity of the service.

Open and Closed Systems

Whether a conservational or a transformational dynamic predominates in a system may often depend on specific temporary circumstances (wars, strikes, changes in leadership, and so on). However, over the long run, the relative predominance of the one or the other in a particular system is a measure of the openness of that system (though not an infallible measure, please note, because a conservational dynamic can appear to predominate even in a highly open system if that system's environment is for some reason unusually stable).

Whether a system is open or closed has to do with the permeability of its boundaries and hence with the degree of its intercommunication or exchange with its environment, including other systems. (For organizations, it is doubtless true that the most essential component of their environment is other organizations.) Given diversity and change in a system's surroundings, the more open the system and the more frequent its external transactions, the more will a transformational dynamic predominate within it. The more closed the system and the more it feeds on itself, the more will a conservational dynamic predominate. A cloistered monastic order would be an organizational example of a relatively closed system, whereas a popular political party would exemplify a relatively open system. However, the latter might be partly closed if control of policy is in the hands of a clique of bosses. Similarly, the monastic order might be quite open to doctrinal inputs from a central church authority.

The approximate quality of these examples shows that the distinction between open and closed systems is a distinction among ideal types. A perfectly open system is a contradiction in terms; it is the absence of a system. Absolutely permeable system boundaries are not boundaries at all and so cannot describe a functional system state. Similarly, a totally closed system, one having no interchange with its environment, could survive only under special conditions (and then probably only briefly) and therefore is unlikely to be encountered in reality. Every system depends on some form of exchange with its environment in order to replenish the resources consumed by the processes of its existence. Without such exchange the system must eventually wither and die.

But even if open or closed systems as pure types are impossible to discover in nature, the distinction between the two is useful both in theory and as an approximation in the practical classification and management of systems. Some organizations are more open than others; some are more oriented toward their environments and concerned with adaptation to them. In short, some organizations are more disposed toward change than are others; how much they are willing to change depends heavily on their openness to external influences.

System Boundaries

Thus another reason why the distinction between open and closed systems is valuable is that it directs attention to the important matter of system boundaries. Without going into detail, the boundaries of systems are defined by discontinuities of time, place, or process. When things are not done at the same time (for example, sleeping and waking), a discontinuity exists between them. When two things are done in different places (assembly of Chevrolet cars in plants in two different cities), there is discontinuity between them. When two activities are different in their modes of performance (washing and ironing a shirt), discontinuities exist. In other words, stops and starts, shifts from place to place, and the things that distinguish one object or person from another on some basis all represent discontinuities. The greater the discontinuity, the more *definite* is the boundary (and, in general, the more closed is the system).

All of the examples given involve some kind of activity, but discontinuities (and hence system boundaries) arise in relation to three main points of organizational reference:

1. *Activities.* The tasks that are performed within the system, to the extent that they are not unitary and absolutely homogenous, provide sources of discontinuity that give rise to system differentiation. For example, teaching and grading examinations, even if done by the same person, are at least partially discontinuous activities; they are different kinds of tasks, rarely performed at the same time. Clerical and custodial functions illustrate the same kind of discontinuity of activity.
2. *Membership.* Discontinuity in perceptions of association, friendship networks, personal identification, and so on give rise to psychological, or what Miller and Rice (1967) call "sentient," system boundaries. A shipping clerk and a secretary included in different activity systems and spatially segregated may nevertheless be friends or belong to the same union and so belong to a common membership system. On the other hand, two middle managers, one a member of the Knights of Columbus and the other a Mason, may regard themselves as belonging to different membership systems. Membership discontinuities can even arise in the context of a single individual. For instance, one of the more interesting organizational puzzles is to define the membership of the shop foreman or first-line supervisor; does he belong to management or to the work group?
3. *Administration.* The organizational designs (departmentalization, physical layout, policies and procedures) according to which systems are operated are the final sources of system boundaries. Ordinarily the psychology departments and physics departments in universities are different organizational

entities, as are medical treatment and surgical units in hospitals. Division of infantry platoons into squads, each having the same function, also illustrates the delineation of administrative boundaries.

Thus it is possible to speak of three general varieties of systems: activity, membership, and organizational (administrative). Instances of each variety will likely be found to some extent in any actual organization (where we would regard them as subsystems of the larger organizational system), but their boundaries may or may not coincide. There are certain problems that arise when system boundaries coincide and others that arise when they do not. A boundary coincidence tends to increase rigidity and so decrease a system's susceptibility to external influence. Nonfraternization rules that ensure coincidence of administrative and sentient system boundaries within the military work to reinforce the distinction between "officers" and "men" and tend to close each system relative to the other.

On the other hand a lack of boundary coincidence can present some sticky problems in managing cross-boundary transactions because organizations naturally tend to adjust their system boundaries in the direction of coincidence. This apparently reflects a kind of simplicity or least-effort principle that requires a consciously planned expenditure of energy to contravene. For example, a university psychology department with which I was associated subdivided itself into specialized areas that represented, among other things, an increased coincidence of activity-system (that is, teaching and research) and administrative-system boundaries. As a result the department resembled a confederation based on subdisciplinary specialties (developmental psychology, social psychology, and so on) more than it did a unitary entity. Each area tended to be segregated, with lowered rates of interaction across area lines and some difficulty in mounting department-wide activities. Just how desirable or undesirable this kind of arrangement might be need not be debated, but neither need it be debated that it would have taken a considerable management effort to sustain a significantly different one.

One conclusion that can be drawn from this review of the various kinds of organizational systems, boundary conditions, interaction patterns, and their associated circumstances is that the sentiments and activities generated within an organization aggregate to guarantee that real-world operating systems will be far more richly textured and refractory to administrative control than traditional organizational charts or official charters and statements of purpose ordinarily suggest. Further, the classical distinction between "formal" and "informal" organizations does only minimal justice to this fact.

Systems within Systems

It follows from the discussion so far that not only are systems differentiated with regard to one another, they are also internally differentiated into specialized parts (subsystems). A gauge of system complexity, and a measure of the managerial challenge presented by an organization, is the degree and variety of subsystem differentiation present. Each organizational subsystem tends to have a psychological correlate in the form of a distinctive frame of reference held by its members. One's view of the organizational mountain, in other words, depends on whether one is at its base or at its summit and on whether one is climbing it or bulldozing it. Simplistic views of organization and administration tend chronically to underestimate the extent of subsystem differentiation and, with it, the degree of organizational complexity, the variety of goals latent in the system, and the magnitude of the managerial challenge. Except by chance, remember, one can hardly administer effectively an organization the nature of which is largely unknown or seriously misunderstood.

The Utility of the System Idea

It seems fair to say that a good manager will try to gain and hold an invigorating institutional perspective on the organization for which he has responsibility. He will try to get a realistic image of the organization as a whole and see its parts in relation. both to one another and to that whole. Indeed, in his doctoral research, Cary M. Lichtman (1968) was able to show a significant association between productivity and knowledge about the employing organization. But the truth is that such perspectives are hard to attain and even harder to sustain. Organizations, after all, are frequently large, complicated, and vague; anyway, they are all full of many little details. One can't see or do everything at once; but it is handy to have a synthetic concept that can at least help to keep one's eye on the doughnut. The great virtue of system notions is that they provide such a concept; they permit a ready transfer of attention from macroscopic institutional references to microscopic part processes and back again. They allow one to see things "whole" and to relate parts to each other in a context of common institutional identity. They remind one of the complexity and interdependencies in organizational phenomena, thereby diminishing temptations to glibness in discussions of the management of such phenomena. At the same time, they provide encouraging means of relating small, seemingly isolated events and changes (in and of themselves possibly trivial) to wider institutional goals and strategies. Thus they supply a base for the rational planning and targeting of resources or change efforts. This application of system notions is illustrated in Chapter 4.

Subsystem Differentiation and Individual Identification

As I have indicated, virtually all systems can be regarded as subsystems of some still larger system. Similarly, any subsystem can be treated as a unit unto itself—that is, as a system. Whether one speaks of a system or a subsystem then depends chiefly on the concerns of the moment and what boundaries one chooses to take as primary. The status of an organization as a system or as a subsystem is principally a matter of definition and convenience, depending on one's focus of attention, special interests, or analytic purposes.

Another point to be made about subsystem differentiation is that, instead of identifying with the organization as a whole, organizational members will tend to identify primarily, if not exclusively, with some subsystem close to their principal occupational or other personal interests. By and large, only higher-level administrative or managerial personnel see the system whole or have what Peter Drucker in 1950 called the "managerial attitude." Consequently, the organization will be perceptually different to different members, depending on their position in it. Moreover, membership in the larger organization will be differently valued as a function of subsystem identifications.

Subsystem identification is not necessarily incompatible with attachment to the larger system. As one first-line supervisor in a federal bureaucracy remarked when queried on this subject, "The Service wants the supervisor's job done, and I want to get it done, so there is no conflict." If a person perceives the fate of a subsystem with which he personally identifies as common with that of the larger system, there is every reason for him to value the larger system (the organization). In fact, this is essentially what Drucker meant by the managerial attitude. The point, however, is that attachment to the organization tends to be mediated by identification with a subsystem and perceptions of the relations between that subsystem and the larger organization. College professors, for instance, frequently identify more firmly with their "profession" or discipline (for example, physics) than with the institution in which they happen to teach. As a result, their job satisfaction is apt to depend on the willingness of institutions to foster the interests of the professor's particular discipline (physics, law, or whatever), and the extent to which faculty membership at a given institution signifies professional attainment. In other words, attachment to the organization commonly is secondary and extrinsic, whereas attachment to the subsystem is primary and intrinsic. There are exceptions to this rule, of course, but don't underestimate the importance of the work group or overestimate direct attachment to the organization. And never assume universality of organizational viewpoint.

LIMITS ON SUBSYSTEM DIFFERENTIATION

The process of decomposing systems into subsystems and, in reverse, of synthesizing systems out of subsystems offers almost infinite possibilities and so may appear to be of little practical value. In a sense, of course, the process is virtually without limit, or at least so "general systems theory" would seem to imply. In practice, however, and certainly in organizational contexts, there are definite functional limitations. Microscopically, subsystem differentiation ceases when no further functionally meaningful distinctions are possible. Macroscopically, the compounding of systems as subsystems of ever-larger systems probably tends to end when exchanges between ostensible subsystems become so difficult that they are reduced in number to a point at which the system lacks substance and is unlikely to be perceived as having the integrity necessary to qualify as a real system.

These rules for defining subsystems are loose and relative, to be sure, but in practice human judgment and consensuses work well enough for most managerial purposes. It is easy, for instance, to see PS 47 as a system or as a subsystem depending on whether you look at it alone (as a system) and at its internal processes or consider it as a component (as a subsystem) of a community's educational establishment. It is simply a matter of the reference points being used. As you progress upward to ever more encompassing levels, this exercise continues to be relatively straightforward until you reach something such as "American society." Debate may go on about exactly where to draw the boundaries, but the largest, most general system normally identifiable will correspond to something familiarly understood as "society." This very general and nearly always highly heterogenous societal system is called the *supersystem.* The important fact about the supersystem is not its status as the grandest system of them all. Its significance lies in its role as the source of the values most widely applicable among the subsystems of which it is composed, which leads to the matter of social norms.

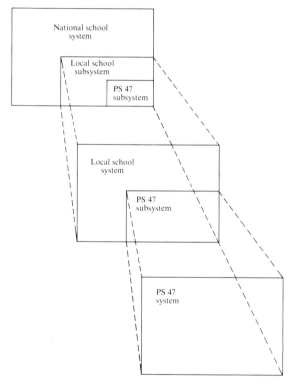

FIGURE 1.   *Representation of PS 47 as a subsystem of larger systems and as a system.*

NORMS

All human systems include an agglomeration of goals, performance routines, etiquette, customs, ethical precepts, and the like; in short, all human systems possess a culture. Each one has a partially distinctive *normative content* that serves to define the particular game it proposes to play and the rules according to which it intends to play the game. Whether openly stated or not, some measure of conformity to these norms is expected of all members as a condition of membership in the system. More generally, because a system's normative content provides an array of criteria for determining the value to the system of various resources and outputs, it may appropriately be used to evaluate the performance (and citizenship) of individual members and to assist decisions concerning recruitment (hiring), continuation of membership (firing), status (promotion), and the distribution of resources (compensation) within a system.

Although no two systems will have exactly the same normative content, some systems will be more similar than others and some norms will be more widely distributed than others. Whether they are absolutely universal or not, the most basic and most general norms are those derived from and defining the supersystem. It is in terms of the normative content (values) of the supersystem (society) that the orientations and operations of its subsystems (specific organizations, for example) must eventually be legitimized. The supersystem, in essence, is the moral frame within which constituent systems operate. It provides the ultimate goals and basic standards of conduct for all its subsystems, both individual and collective. Just as the normative contents of individual systems such as organizations provide standards against which to measure performance of their individual members, so do the norms of the supersystem provide criteria for the assessment of subsystems as units. In other words, norms provide criteria for measuring the effectiveness of subsystems. It is on premises like these that Talcott Parsons (1951) rests his argument that profit making cannot be the *primary* goal of business enterprise because it lacks broad *social* legitimacy and is insufficiently moral. In any event, these ideas allow derivation of a general model for evaluating systems and hence a way of arriving at judgments of organizational effectiveness: every system or subsystem is a unit in a larger system; the performance of each such unit may be evaluated in terms of the normative content of the relevant system, with the norms of the supersystem being applicable to all. Thus individuals may be evaluated in relation to organizational criteria, but organizations may also be evaluated according to societal criteria. And, of course, all sorts of intermediate levels of evaluation are possible.

Evaluating Organizations as Systems and Subsystems

The point of my story up to now is that a system-type perspective encourages at least two distinct ways of looking at organizations; each is relevant to problems of how to increase organizational effectiveness. On the one hand, it is pertinent to look on organizations, individually or collectively, from the viewpoint of a "conservational mode of analysis"—so-called because its emphasis is on the essential conservation of the system's traditional principles. On the other hand, managers can employ a "transformational mode of analysis" that begins by calling into question the organization's social-value premises.

A conservational mode of analysis treats organizations as unitary entities—that is, as self-contained systems. Attention focuses mainly on their manifest structural and internal properties. *Efficency* (productivity) and *morale* are the chief touchstones of interest from such a conservational vantage point. In other words, organizational output is considered mainly in relation to the "work" of the organization (its task functions) and the happiness of its participants (its maintenance functions). The output standards or normative criteria according to which judgments about morale and efficiency have usually been made in the particular organization, however, are not themselves in question. In fact they are treated as given.

A conservational analysis of an organization stresses ways of improving the organization with regard to existing standards, increasing its effectiveness by making it better at doing basically what it has always done. Such analysis also has the effect of preserving the interests and patterns of relations that the system has always preserved (although change in patterns of relations is not necessarily precluded, especially if it is determined that their alteration might increase productivity).

Input-Output Analysis

A convenient and comparatively simple way to implement this orientation (which can, of course, be made highly technical and sophisticated) is by seeking improvement in the relationship between input and output events. To improve this relationship requires identification of the output events (staff morale, fees earned, failure rates in specified courses, hospital-bed turnover, widgets produced per man-day, net changes in welfare caseload, and so forth) on which attention can center. Output targets (those goods or services—outcomes—that the system will strive to generate) will not always be the same, as we have seen. Moreover, respect for the limitations of the information-processing capabilities of the system and especially of people is essential; no effort should be made to do everything at once. If the system is in such disrepair that total remedy is re-- quired, then it is probably time to junk it anyway and start anew.

Selection of output targets is only part of the review process. Criteria for evaluating output must be determined. This requires reasonably clear elucidation of the system's goals, both generally and in a fashion that highlights appropriate output targets. How an organization states its goals defines the basic criteria it will use for evaluating its outputs. Outputs, in turn, reflect on the processes by which they are produced. These processes are the nucleus of the productivity problem and constitute the essence of what is often called "management by objectives."

Determining output targets and system goals is a necessary step in a review-and-development process. Such determination will identify the end items or events that the system will be oriented toward generating and will provide an explicit evaluation framework for the system's outputs. But targets, goals, and evaluation frameworks have to be transformed into practicable procedures if they are to have any concrete meaning. Acceptable ways of measuring output need to be elaborated, and means must be found for monitoring changes in the performance subsystems that yield those outputs. This last matter directs attention to the input events on which output depends. A careful inventory of input events relative to each output target is a necessary preliminary to assessment and improvement of performance.

Generally speaking, inputs can be classified as technical, personal, or organizational.* Collectively, they define the resources actually or potentially available to the system, and they determine

---

*John A. Seiler has suggested a classification similar to the one used here (adding norms and structure as a fourth input). In fact, he largely organizes his book *Systems Analysis in Organizational Behavior* (1967) around this discussion.

the system's output. Careful analysis of their nature and combination in relation to the requirements of selected output targets can sometimes reveal, *a priori,* the shape of reforms needed to improve system performance (for example, upgrading personnel-skill levels, obtaining more production resources, reallocating resources via budget changes, improving control over resource use, and so on). More often, however, a more empirical-experimental, trial-and-error approach will be necessary; a fact that highlights the critical need to develop methods for measuring and monitoring performance events.

At any rate, *technical inputs* are those having to do mainly with "hardware" and its underlying technology. They include the physical setting of the system, its machinery, and its access to relevant information systems. Technical inputs plainly mesh intimately with personal inputs having to do with skills. The latter could as easily be classified as technical, leaving to the "personal" category exclusively those attributes conventionally associated with human personality. I have classified skills as personal inputs because, although they are perhaps expressions of technology, they are manifest in personal form where their use is a matter of motivation.

Personal (or personnel) inputs then have to do with the attitudes, sentiments, aptitudes, and skills extant within the system and with such routine matters as number, age, and sex of employees. In this connection, the word "personal" is preferred to "personnel" because I wish to emphasize the *functions* involved, not the individuals. In effective organizational performance, as I said earlier, the availability and distribution of characteristics (resources) within the system are at issue—not the concrete persons who manifest them.

How the resources available within a system may be brought to bear on an output target is an "organizational" rather than a "personal" problem. It may, for instance, require the pooling of individuals and/or their multiple deployment within the system instead of customary individual and exclusive assignments. Familiar examples of this are the team-teaching concept in schools, the nurse-administrator in hospitals, the creation of project organizations, and, in this book, the use of work supervisors as counselors. I merely suggest the formalization and extension of this principle. Personal inputs have to do with the availability of needed resources within the system. Should they be lacking, the system will need to recruit them from outside, develop them internally (via in-service training) or else transform its objectives to correspond with the personal resources that are available. These problems are fundamentally *organizational.*

Failure to recognize this fact has bedeviled many of the approaches to organization development that have sometimes inclined toward preoccupation with persons and personalities and lost sight of the other inputs and processes that combine with personality to yield system outputs.

Organizational inputs, then, refer to the structures, policies, and procedures by which the system operates. They have to do with the purposeful pattern according to which the system works to accomplish its ends. This pattern represents the organization's functional solutions to the problems it confronts and its ways of relating its personal and technical resources to its output targets. Obviously, therefore, these inputs* are crucial to the success and adaptability of the system, for it is a matter not merely of what resources are available to the system but of how they are used and how they are related to and coordinated with output targets. Solzhenitsyn's recent book, *August 1914* (1971) vividly depicts how, despite overwhelming superiority in manpower, the Russian army in East Prussia managed to accomplish catastrophic defeat during World War I by incompetent deployment of its resources. As history has repeatedly shown and as the "Peter Principle" affirms (Peter, 1969), a man in one position might be a disaster; in another, a blessing. I should note, too, that as a managerial enterprise, organizational inputs relate to the maintenance and implementation of nearly all the operations with which I have been or will be concerned here. The coherent combination of technical, personal, and organizational inputs in fact constitutes what I called in Chapter 1, "the technology-structure-policy nexus of organization."

An especially vital organizational input is the forging of *role networks* for the accomplishment of the system's goals. Organizations operate via complex dynamic interaction processes, and roles describe the fundamental coalescence of technical, personal, and organizational inputs around more or less clearly specified functional objectives or output targets. Final evaluation of system performance and the basic focus for its improvement center on the effectiveness of role networks because, in effect, these constitute the organization's rules for resource allocation and use. I shall return to this in a later chapter.

---

*The actual implementation of plans, policies, programs, and what have you, are often referred to as "processes" rather than inputs. In this chapter I am generally dispensing with that kind of distinction, although in later chapters I shall find them worthwhile, especially as regards matters such as managerial "styles."

In *summary* of this portion of the discussion, the essential components of input-output analysis are:

1. Selection of output targets.
2. Determination of criteria for evaluation of outputs.
3. Determination of means for measuring and monitoring performance.
4. Review of system resources available for use as inputs to organizational operation.
5. Assessment of input-output relations, the system's role network.

This mode of analysis concentrates on institutional conservation and reform (or improvement) with reference to traditional values. It does not encourage searching critique of goals, standards, or normative contents; instead, it stresses methods. There is much to be said for it as a type of analysis; indeed there is no substitute for it. However, it requires a complementary mode of analysis if review of an organization's effectiveness is to be complete. Exclusive devotion to customary issues of efficiency and morale rarely leads to serious questioning of traditional goals and standards or to a search for alternatives. Worse, it fosters a kind of organizational way of life that leads to a great deal of structural tinkering, bureaucratic proliferation, and tendencies to close system boundaries, thereby isolating the organization from the broader world. An antidote for these toxic happenings is to look at the organization as a social institution, as a subsystem of society. Doing so demands that you become concerned with definition of the organization's social functions by looking closely at its explicit and implicit values and examining the social and human justifications for its traditional criteria for evaluating outputs. The growing (if often grudging) emphasis among American businesses on "social responsibility" and the stress on "accountability" among public organizations such as schools illustrate such examination. In other words, instead of attending strictly or even chiefly to the effectiveness of individual or subgroup performance with a stable and perhaps traditional matrix of goals and methods, organizational performance can receive more dynamic review by reference to the larger normative nexus on which its legitimacy rests. This normative review process sometimes is spoken of with a faint touch of overstatement as "social auditing."

The Process of Goal Selection

The change-oriented transformational posture stresses not only goal setting but also the more exacting requirements of goal evaluation and goal selection with reference to general value systems. Concerned with convergences and divergences between the system's premises and those of the larger society, transformational analysis encourages consideration of the contribution of subsystems to the attainment of overarching system objectives and fosters study of the system's comprehensive relations with its social-moral milieu. If done seriously, such analyses can stimulate healthy dialogue about the nature and modes of implementation of societal standards and procedures within the system, thereby fulfilling an honorable and essential organizational responsibility to critique, as well as advance, the society of which the system is a part. By asking how effective the organization is in fulfilling its societal role, the transformational mode of organizational analysis begins to provide a rational living base for a *selection* of social norms and for the adjudication and constructive use of the conflict that even Warren Bennis (1970) has come to see as endemic to organizations.

There are, to be sure, dangers in exclusive reliance on a transformational orientation, just as there are in its conservational analog. For one thing, preoccupation with goals may foster a disregard for the means of their attainment. The blithe belief that formulating a goal is tantamount to its achievement sometimes gains currency. From his experiences, one school administrator, Robert L. Farkas, who happens also to have been one of my more stimulating students, has put the matter this way:

1. In those school systems that have formalized the goal-setting process, the results of the effort may be found in the bottom drawer of the chief school officer's or principal's file cabinet sandwiched between reports on the nutritional aspects of Class A lunches and the cost-effectiveness study of sheet versus roll lavatory tissue.
2. School system goals are global statements that defy measurement.
3. School system goals are generally not promulgated to the professional staff, and in those cases where they do reach the staff and/or community they merely become sandwiched between a different set of papers.

4. Subjectivity in interpretation results in a number of interpretations equal to those reviewing the goals.

[This] exercise in hyperbole is tempered by the fact that an increasing number of school systems are engaged in a sincere effort to acquire expertise in the development of behavioral objectives. Although still at the stage of a humble beginning, it appears that honest professional interest and accountability pressure speed the process.*

One might choose to repose more confidence in the second rather than the first item mentioned by Dr. Farkas. In any case, appearances to the contrary notwithstanding, the circumstances depicted are most assuredly not confined to educational organizations.

The transformational posture also has another danger: it can spawn a conviction that any method that achieves the goal is acceptable. The fact is that some means are patently better than others. Earlier in this chapter I commented that decisions about organizational effectiveness needed to be broadly based, that they needed to take into account many goals and possible side effects. Side effects arise from the unanticipated consequences of goal achievement and from the system's reactions to the methods or processes by which goal achievement is pursued. Some processes are more economical than others in consumption of material resources or result in less wear and tear on the morale of organization members. Thus an effective organization not only achieves its objectives but achieves them via efficient means. Further, it is no mere platitude to say that the end does not justify the means.

To restate the argument, then, analyses of organizations as self-contained entities on the one hand and as social institutions on the other are complementary modes essential to a comprehensive review of system performance. Viewing the organization or organizational element as a subsystem of a broader organizational or societal system is both an origin and a terminus for general system development. Intermeshed with something like input-output analysis, a fully realized approach to the enhancement of system effectiveness (in-

---

*R. Farkas, Determining criteria for organizational effectiveness. Unpublished manuscript, 1971. Used by permission of the author.

cluding its moral quality) can result.* I have said before, however, that actual accomplishment of this objective requires motivation on the part of system members to work for the system's improvement. Unfortunately, such motivation may be problematical—an issue to which we now turn.

Productivity and Organizational Effectiveness: Problems of Motivation

In his book *The New Industrial State* (1972), John Kenneth Galbraith offers the trenchant observation that organizational effectiveness results from a meaningful meshing of disparate intraorganizational goals. It follows that organizational effectiveness will be at least a partial function of the degree of consensus that exists among organization members regarding the organization's goals. (Other things such as knowledge or skill and the state of the environment may also be involved.) But, as I have pointed out, it is not always true that all members of particular organizations have the same goals or share a common "mission identification." If they do not, then what can effectiveness mean? Does it mean the number of units of something produced in some time period? Does it mean the "quality" of those units? Does it mean the "acclaim" the organization has received? Does it mean the reputations of the organization's members? Does it mean any of these, some of these, all of these, other things, or what? Since, as a generality, questions of productivity boil down to how well the organization does its job, guaranteeing at least some general agreement on that subject is plainly essential to progress. This does not mean that everyone must have the same goals, nor does it mean that an organization's goals must never change. What it does mean is that goals need to be congruent and not mutually incompatible. Most important, the system's goals must be widely

*Although the idea is not emphasized here, the kind of institutional critique outlined can be extended to encompass larger societal questions about managing the "organizational revolution" discussed in Chapter 1. Assuring social equity and being saved from what Perrow (1972) somewhat melodramatically termed the "selfish ravages" of powerful organizations depends on detailed scrutiny of organizational and interorganizational transactions in societal perspective. Who benefits? If genuine concern exists for the general welfare, this is a necessary and natural question.

credible, acceptable, and harmonious with individual and subsystem goals.

But, once again, achieving clarity and understanding about goals must not be confused with goal realization. People must still be motivated to belong to the organization, to seek its goals, and to accept its methods. Whether they will depends on their perceptions of whether the system actually seems to be working toward its goals and what degree of equity for the members results from its outputs. To repeat, for people to be motivated to attach themselves to an organization and accept its goals and work for them, they must believe in the organization and perceive their interests to be linked with its interests and to be served by its conduct. Whether the conditions necessary to assure this are present in many contemporary organizations is questionable, which is why the matter of motivation is so often problematical in organizations.

Subsystems and Subsystems

Organizations often fail to earn genuine commitment from their members because they elaborate within themselves many only tangentially related subsystems. Most of these subsystems are unlikely to be revealed in an ordinary organizational chart, but together they greatly affect what happens in the organization and go a long way toward impairing organizational effectiveness by vitiating the organization's ability to motivate individual attachment. One of these subsystems includes the organization's top management and may be called the *executive subsystem*. Nourished by traditional conceptions of its inalienable prerogatives, this subsystem is typically organized with an array of structures (subsystems) and norms, many of which are informal or only tacitly understood. These structures and norms are elaborated relative to and consistent with the distinctive special interests of executives.*

---

*Especially crass instances of this are widely reputed to occur in the military. They include the special status and opportunity for promotion that West Pointers supposedly enjoy in the Army and commendations for valor in combat that lead to decorations and career advancement but that are allegedly known to be false or exaggerated by confirming officers (who expect the same favors in return). So-called "congressional junketing" also falls in this category, as does the abuse of "executive privilege" with which President Nixon was accused, presumably as a way of concealing misdeeds by his powerful assistants who many believed tended to treat the United States government as their own instrument quite without regard for the "will of the people."

To express and safeguard their own interests, other subsystems in turn develop their own distinctive structures and cultures. At certain obvious junctures these various subsystems make contact and exchange resources. However, much of the life of the larger system (the organization) takes place *within*, not among, these semiclosed subsystems, and the "official" goals of the total system may never be accomplished. Moreover, the potential for competition and conflict is obvious.

Understandably, organizational subsystems strive to arrange things to yield at least a reasonable degree of special comfort to themselves. As a result, the real tasks to which the system is functionally oriented come to be synthesized in a crucible of divergent interests. Cyert and March (1963) had this in mind when they described organizations as collections of coalitions and characterized their processes in terms of negotiation, bargaining, and conflict. Because certain subsystems tend to be more powerful and to dominate the larger system's processes and outputs, the organization can become effectively transformed into a system peculiarly adapted to benefit a particular subsystem—fourteenth-century monarchies being only extreme examples. The further result is that the organization's "work" is precluded from being a collaborative venture and degenerates into an implicit or explicit power struggle. We are concerned in this book with some ways of at least "deescalating" that struggle, because the kind of subsystem divergence just described tends to prevent accomplishment of overall organizational effectiveness. Power struggles dissipate resources, and concentration on single subsystems can lead to their aggrandizement at the expense of the organization as a whole.

Summary of System Perspectives on Organizational Effectiveness

In this chapter, I have presented a view of organizations as complex social systems. I have construed organizational output as being the product of an interplay of people—or, more exactly, their characteristics—and the structures that pattern their relations. I pictured organizations as internally diverse with different membership groupings (subsystems), each seeking more or less distinctive goals. I depicted the organization as competing with other organizations to obtain the resources (inputs) necessary to maintenance and performance.

I also described two complementary modes of organizational analysis corresponding to the conservational and transformational tendencies of human systems. The conservational mode of analysis concentrates on the organization as a self-contained entity and on "making the system better at doing what it always has done." This mode is thus oriented essentially toward the status quo. A change-oriented transformational mode of analysis on the other hand treats the particular organization as a subsystem of the larger societal super-system and applies to its appraisal the "citizenship" values of the larger society. Put briefly, the conservational mode of analysis mainly asks questions about the organization's *efficiency* as a resource-using system, whereas a transformational mode of analysis asks about the organization's *morality* as a resource-using system. Together these two modes of analysis represent a comprehensive approach to assessing the "effectiveness" of organizations.

With respect to effectiveness itself, I pointed out that an organization can be said to have goals (or to have goals set for it) and that statement of those goals amounts to specification of the targets to which the system's resources are to be allocated. Goal statements also represent normative criteria for evaluating the organization's performance (including the policies by which resources are selected and allocated). However, organizational effectiveness should not be thought of as simple goal achievement. The complexity and diversity of organizations, together with their fluidity as open human systems, preclude the selection of single particular objectives as final criteria of organizational effectiveness.

I have characterized an effective organization as one that has attained a bargaining position in its operating environment that allows it to obtain the resources it needs for the activities in which it chooses to engage. How well the organization defines its needs and how carefully it arranges strategies and tactics for need satisfaction are, therefore, major multidimensional questions for management to raise in trying to assure the success of the organization. An organization is effective to the degree that it can survive and control its own fate, which depends on its capability as a resource-getting system that can more often than not satisfy both the variable requirements for its performance and also the needs of its individual members.

The contemporary organization plainly faces a sizable set of hard-to-solve problems. Social roles are complicated and ill-defined.

More and more, organizational membership is wildly heterogenous. Pressures have mounted somehow to relate organizational performance ever more completely to the needs and interests of a society uncertain of its own objectives. To grapple meaningfully with these issues, the modern manager must seek new ways of motivating more effective performance by melding heretofore disjunctive or competing organizational subsystems into mutually supportive, if not coincident, systems. The era is past when the members of a dominant management subsystem could deal with the members of subordinate (and presumably passive) subsystems as if to fabricate some item of hardware from inanimate raw materials.

The fact is that societal thrusts toward a wider sharing of power and more authentic participation in policy-making can hardly be expected to exempt any particular species of organization—nor should they. Paternalism, no matter how well-intentioned, is anachronistic in the present world. Making organizations more effective is a matter first and foremost of a broadly based critique of their goals, nominal and real, and of their modes of operation as task-oriented systems. Such critique provides a basis for the development and implementation of operational and managerial methods than can facilitate the performance of organizational goals. Efforts to encourage more effective organizational performance must be particular to specific organizations and their missions. However, there are general principles, attitudes, and practices that are widely applicable as guides to effective managerial conduct. Chapter 3 begins the description of these guides by stating a basic orientation to the nature and functions of management in organizations.

References

Bennis, W. G. A funny thing happened on the way to the future. *American Psychologist*, 1970, **25,** 595–609.

Cyert, R. M., & March, J. G. *A behavioral theory of the firm.* New York: Prentice-Hall, 1963.

Drucker, P. *The new society.* New York: Harper & Row, 1962.

Farkas, R. L. The determining criteria for organizational effectiveness. Unpublished manuscript, State University of New York at Buffalo, 1972.

Galbraith, J. K. *The new industrial state.* (2nd ed.) San Jose, Calif.: H. M. Gousha, 1972.

Katz, D., & Kahn, R. L. *The social psychology of organizations.* New York: John Wiley & Sons, 1966.

Lichtman, C. M. An interactional analysis of structural and individual variables in a work organization. Unpublished doctoral dissertation, State University of New York at Buffalo, 1968.

Miller, E. J., & Rice, A. K. *Systems of organization.* London: Tavistock Publications, 1967.

Parsons, T. *The social system.* New York: Free Press, 1951.

Perrow, C. *Complex organizations: A critical essay.* Glenview, Ill.: Scott Foresman, 1972.

Peter, L. J. *The Peter principle.* New York: Morrow, 1969.

Seiler, J. A. *Systems analysis in organizational behavior.* Homewood, Ill.: Irwin-Dorsey, 1967.

Solzhenitsyn, A. *August 1914.* New York: Farrar, Straus & Giroux, 1971.

Yuchtman, E., & Seashore, S. E. A system resource approach to organizational effectiveness. *American Sociological Review,* 1967, **32,** 891–903.

Recommended Readings

Banton, M. *Roles: An introduction to the study of social relations.* New York: Basic Books, 1965. (An exceptionally lucid, deceptively simple presentation of role concepts and their value in social analysis.)

Cleland, D. I., & King, W. R. *Systems analysis and project management.* New York: McGraw-Hill, 1968. (An excellent, nonmathematical presentation of basic concepts.)

Hunt, R. G. Technology and organization. *Academy of Management Journal,* 1970, **13,** 235–253. (A discussion of ways of classifying organizations, the nature of technology, and relations between technology and organizational structures.)

Lichtman, C. M., & Hunt, R. G. Personality and organization theory. *Psychological Bulletin,* 1971, **76,** 271–294. (A review of various organizational schools of thought that have to do with the importance attached to structural as opposed to personality variables in determining outcomes. The authors try to show the integrative potential of system and role concepts.)

Mouzelis, N. P. *Organization and bureaucracy: An analysis of modern theories.* Chicago: Aldine-Atherton, 1967. (A useful, brief but wide-ranging treatment of bureaucracy and other views of organization.)

Odiorne, G. S. *Management by objectives.* New York: Pitman, 1965. (A readable presentation of concepts and techniques by one of the principals in the field.)

Olson, M. E. *The process of social organization.* New York: Holt, Rinehart & Winston, 1968. (An excellent, if demanding, general sociological treatment of basic organization concepts, theories, and phenomena. Concrete organizational entities are treated as instances of more general social processes.)

chapter
three

A Philosophy
for Management

We have seen that the tasks and responsibilities of management have changed as a result of changes in the wider world of work. Even in the face of increased specialization, the variety of functions for which today's manager has responsibility has grown considerably. Especially affected have been those difficult "unprogrammed" problem-solving activities falling outside the scope of specific technical performance routines.

More significant than the enlargement of managerial roles is the fact that the various managerial functions have undergone a reordering of priority. As separate strands, even the most familiar management functions now are woven into administrative roles according to designs quite different from traditional ones. From these two related developments, a new image of management has emerged; this image calls for a managerial outlook suited to it and special skills to assure its fulfillment.

Newer Perspectives on Management

Current views of the nature of organizations stress their conceptualization as dynamic open social systems. The basic units of organization are to be found among the networks of human relationships in which and through which the work of the enterprise takes place and the system itself becomes interconnected with its surrounding environment. Organizational processes become manifest in the complex of sometimes subtle reciprocal social or interpersonal influences. Although they may not wholly determine them, these influences nonetheless affect profoundly the directions and outcomes of organizational activity. To look on the manager narrowly and mechanistically as a mere organizer and overseer of work is simply not sufficient. The framework of modern social change and our growing understanding of organizational processes combine to make such simplistic notions about management literally dangerous. Redefinition and meaningful expansion of managerial roles have become necessary.

Abstractly, the functions of management may be broadly described as finding ways for somehow guiding the enterprise toward achievement of its goals, however variously those goals may be defined. In practice, this grand objective decomposes into a myriad specialized, limited, and particular part-goals that combine to specify the day-to-day work requirements of management. These include organizing and overseeing work, but they include more than that.

Responsibility for guaranteeing achievement of particular subgoals may be functionally and hierarchically distributed within the system. Every manager, at whatever organizational level, will be charged with getting some more or less specific job done. Frequently, in fact, the manager believes that his role and his understanding of the organization's overall objectives are based on his special task function exclusively. With such a viewpoint, the manager tends to adopt a foreshortened time perspective and to equate final organizational objectives with subsystem part-goals. This will be recognized as the what's-good-for-General-Motors-is-good-for-the-country syndrome. Moreover, he becomes straightjacketed into a limited technical understanding of his role and a preoccupation with immediate output criteria for performance. Such mental states are hardly calculated to facilitate high-level organizational operation. To optimize the system's functioning, ideally each manager and supervisor should be able to see the system more or less whole, be able to perceive the relationship of his particular functions to a larger pattern of organizational activity, and be able to understand needs other than his own or his department's. In short, every manager needs to have a managerial attitude.

The Functions of Managers

In the previous chapter, I pointed out that, as a system, every organization requires resources both for its maintenance and for its performance. Supplying maintenance and performance inputs thus defines the dual functions of management's concrete agents—the individual managers. Task performance is of undeniable organizational importance, but getting the job done depends fundamentally on the sustained existence of the organization as a viable operating system. The manager has an obvious and well-recognized responsibility for the performance of tasks, but he must also be willing and able to broaden the compass of his concerns and contribute to the maintenance and even the enhancement of the organization. Not one but two broad functions or requirements can, therefore, be identified for management: *task functions and system maintenance* (including so-called social-emotional functions).

Task functions can be interpreted, for present purposes, as having to do with the particular "business" of an organization—its work. Microscopically, the task functions (work) of an organization will vary widely, all the way from the production of space capsules to the administration of social-security programs, the instruction of children, and the fomenting of revolution. As an organization differentiates its primary tasks into distinct components or subtasks, responsibility for their separate enactment (and coordination) may be allocated to permanent or impermanent work groups. Certain skill mixes will then ordinarily define their particular tasks more microscopically.

For instance, in a survey-research organization, the primary task for the organization as a whole—"the task that it must perform to survive" (Rice, 1963)—may be construed as implementing field-research programs. Doing that involves performance of a great variety of distinctive subtasks (sampling, field interviewing, keypunching, computer programming, bookkeeping, and so on). Responsibility for performance of these component tasks is assigned to particular organizational subunits (for example, Field Division, Technical Services, or Project Manager). Field Division, say, then defines its tasks, primary and other, in terms of those responsibilities allocated to it: consultation on instrument design and field strategies, recruiting and training data collectors, assigning and supervising field operations, and other similar duties. To assure integration and coordination of tasks across performance sectors, the Survey Research Center at the State University of New York at Buffalo has a chief of operations at the organization level and, at the project level, project directors, as well as general management structures and provision for policy guidance of its activities.

The point here is that, no matter what they may be or how they may be understood or what their relations are with other systems, task functions are characteristic of social systems. They may not always be equally stressed among all varieties of social systems (tasks are more prominent and more sharply etched in what we term work organizations than they are in such organizational systems as sororities), but task functions are nevertheless organizational universals. Hence responsibility for their performance is omnipresent among managers.

The second organizational function, system maintenance, has to do with obtaining and using the resources necessary for the general coherence and stability of the enterprise. Just as an organization must attend to its work, so must it retain, recruit, develop, and otherwise secure the material and human resources necessary to its present performance and future operation. No organization can long survive in the face of inattention to either of these two functional requirements. Neither can it suffer more than occasional incompetence in their handling. Over the long run, task and maintenance functions are clearly of equal importance to the organization, even though, in the short run, emphases may fluctuate from one to the other and their immediate importance may vary with circumstances in the environment of the system.

In this book, I emphasize aspects of system maintenance that have to do with the organization's human resources and the system's relationship to the larger societal supersystem. Of central concern are questions of organizational social responsibility and managerial responsibilities associated with what Katz and Kahn described as "holding the human parts in the system and mobilizing their energies in prescribed patterns. . . ." Issues of morale and organizational effectiveness measured against human and social criteria are fundamental matters. As a result, attention fastens on what have come to be called the social-emotional functions of leadership.

There is a risk in attending mainly to social-emotional functions, for it must be kept in mind that the maintenance functions of management are not defined exclusively in social-emotional terms. It is a risk worth taking, however, because I believe that management's maintenance functions are primarily definable in such terms. Put differently, I would suggest that managerial maintenance operations will be generally more successful for being conceptualized and organized so that social-emotional considerations form their nucleus.

The same things are true, I believe, of task functions. Managers certainly do have responsibility for production. Classical scientific management approaches to organizational processes were limited by a preoccupation with task functions. In the same way, the human-relations school was limited because, in its social-emotional reformist zeal, it lost sight of task requirements. The system perspective on organizations (and the counseling orientation), however, provides a way of conceptualizing the managerial role on premises of human and social responsibility so as to incorporate task and maintenance components.

MANAGERIAL FUNCTIONS, MANAGERIAL STYLE, AND SUPERVISORY CLIMATES

What supervisors do on their jobs is fundamental to diagnoses of the climate of supervision within the system. However, there is also a stylistic aspect of role performance. *What* supervisors and managers do is only part of the story. *How* they do it defines the atmosphere of supervision.

Unfortunately, precisely what is meant by supervisory style is not so clear as we might wish or imagine. Still, one thing that can be said about it is that it has more to do with general approaches, emphases, and attitudes toward supervisory tasks than it has to do with specifics of behavior or performance. Two supervisors could *do* pretty much the same thing (in the sense of performing the same tasks), but each can manifest a different *style* in doing it. Two foremen might both assign and monitor work, review performance, troubleshoot, receive grievances, and so on, and yet impress their subordinates very differently. I have found, too, that style can be an extremely subtle thing. In one study on the psychiatric service of a general hospital, I found two head nurses, both of whom described their roles in almost identical terms. Both were characterized by their subordinates as technically "well-qualified" and as "lenient about enforcing rules." Nevertheless, they were very differently evaluated on a respect-nonrespect scale, mainly because one was perceived as being motivated by her concern for the welfare of her subordinates and patients, whereas the other was perceived as being motivated by an acute sense of her own convenience.

Thus the way a particular manager understands and enacts his role expresses what is called his style. Although it is often difficult in actual practice to obtain the measurements needed for rigorous description, managerial styles may be defined operationally in terms of the emphases a manager puts on task as opposed to maintenance functions.

Robert Blake, for instance, proposes that style be thought of as varying along two independent continuous dimensions: "concern for people" and "concern for production" (Blake & Mouton, 1969). By selecting scale points and relating persons simultaneously to both dimensions, Blake is able to describe an array of supervisory orientations or theories that are then symbolized in terms of numerical managerial ratings on the two stylistic dimensions (for example, 1,1; 1,5; and 9,1). Blake believes that supervisory style (and, as a result, organizational performance) is optimized under a theory or approach maximizing both people and production dimensions (9,9 in Blake's notation).

At the University of Michigan, Rensis Likert (1961) has stated a somewhat similar thesis. He elects, however, to speak of "work-centered" versus "employee-centered" styles of management. Likert characterizes work-centered leadership styles as involving "concentration on keeping . . . subordinates busily engaged in . . . a specified work cycle in a prescribed way and at a satisfactory rate as determined by time standards." On the other hand, employee-centered styles "focus . . . on the human aspects of . . . subordinates' problems and on endeavoring to build effective work groups with high performance standards." More recently, Likert (1967) has described managerial styles as complex clusters of activities ranging on a continuum from what he labels System 1 to System 4, the latter denoting a generally optimal mix of operational work and people emphases. Likert has especially stressed motivational strategies and group-oriented tactics in his discussions of how to go about developing more effective organizations based on employee-centered management.

It may be argued that, because organizations are open social systems, two-dimensional models such as Blake's and Likert's yield imperfect views of global managerial postures. They pay insufficient attention to what Warren Bennis (Bennis & Slater, 1968) has singled out as the pre-eminent managerial need for regulating organization-environment adaptations. But, in any case, Blake and Likert's models have great merit if for no other reason than because they stress the fundamental organizational significance of both maintaining system membership and sustaining high levels of performance. Furthermore, both models (and others like them) show that high levels of morale are not necessarily inconsistent with high production standards. At the same time, production and morale are distinct organizational objectives, and achievement of the one in no way guarantees automatic achievement of the other.

Of Men, Machines, and Motivation

Earlier ideas about management tended to emphasize task functions to the virtual exclusion of maintenance functions. Development of efficient work routines was the touchstone and nearly exclusive preoccupation of so-called "machine models" of management. The organizational and managerial premises associated, for example, with Frederick Taylor's "scientific management" (aptly called "physiological organization theory" by James March and Herbert Simon [1958]) tended to see the optimization of work systems as chiefly a matter of developing mechanical performance routines based on standards derived from time-and-motion studies. A worker's motivation to perform was, for Taylor, essentially a moral matter, tacitly assumed on an all-or-none basis. The worker was "switched on" and, like a machine, emitted a determinate flow of work. Variations in output, according to this viewpoint, were almost wholly a function of the efficiency of the performance routines "scientifically" designed into the system. I have called this an earlier view, but the fact is that it has by no means disappeared from the managerial scene. In fact, it may well dominate management in one form or another. The executive describing the goals of his company as "to make a profit, *period*" is neither atypical nor far removed from a kind of proto-Taylorism. And the same is true of the modern technocrat who believes that the tools of operations research define the sum total of managerial wisdom.

Taylor's ideas were not so much wrong as they were biased and incomplete. Later, organizations that had human-relations-oriented ideas of administration began similarly, if contrastingly, to concern themselves almost as narrowly with enhancing workers' job satisfaction. They believed occupational satisfaction, in and of itself, to be a valid social objective, but they also blithely trusted that happy employees would be productive employees. Though one-sided, the human-relations school did serve to spotlight the human side of enterprise and to direct attention to worker motivation as a fundamental organizational variable.

Organizations that have newer ideas about organization and management try to balance and integrate interest in the performance of task functions and interest in morale into a comprehensive conception of system performance through time. Among other things, this integration has led to the emergence of explicit motivational theories of management, which include these two coequal responsibilities of managers:

1. Motivating people to join and remain with the organization. (This will be recognized as the morale or system-maintenance function, the "people" dimension of organization.)
2. Motivating people to produce at high levels. (This is the task function, the "work" dimension.)

The difficulty of implementing both of these responsibilities at the same time can hardly be doubted. It may even be doubted whether both can be simultaneously maximized, at least by the same individual. But, since *both* are nonetheless essential to organizational operation and survival, some satisfactory organizational accommodation to them must be found. The search for means for such accommodation has focused attention on the "vital motivational processes by which persons become attached to organizations and, once they are attached, are prompted to perform in them" (Hollander & Hunt, 1971, p. 556).

ORGANIZATIONAL EFFECTIVENESS

Appreciation of the primary motivational features of functioning organizations and the consequent responsibilities of managers is thus prerequisite to effective individual and organizational performance. Galbraith (1967), with characteristic pith, has put it this way: "What is called an effective organization is one which, in substantial measure, has a motivational system that is internally reinforcing. The goals of the organization are thus pursued with the greatest possible effect" (p. 132). When the man on the assembly line, the girl in the office, and the old gentleman in accounting all see overlap in their interests and harmony with what they understand to be the organization's objectives, everybody tends to pull together and the system is well on the road to effective operation. Therefore, it is management's responsibility to motivate performances that will be instrumental in achieving organizational goals. To do that, however, managers somehow need to persuade the organization's members of the personal legitimacy, relevance, and desirability of the organization's goals. Success in performing this function, when mixed with appropriate technical skills, organizational structures, and work routines, can be expected to result in a more effective organization—an organization wherein disparities between individual and organizational goal structures are minimized and the efficiency of performance programs is maximized.

Merely defining an effective organization (as I did in Chapter 2) is no guarantee of its achievement, especially when balancing task and maintenance functions is so delicate a job. Indeed, what managers have typically done about their motivational responsibilities is to ignore them or else to rely on the supposed motivational muscle of money or the use of authority, threats, and punishment to compel performance. However, there is reason to doubt the universal potency of money as a motivator and even better reason to believe that compulsion is inefficient and self-defeating over the long run.

REWARD VERSUS PUNISHMENT AS WAYS OF CONTROLLING BEHAVIOR

Punishment (and the threat of it) is among the most common and time-honored of all techniques used to influence behavior. The pattern of its use is familiar and ubiquitous: if a man fails to behave as we wish, we threaten to knock him down or to fire him; if a child misbehaves, we spank him; if the people or government of a country become unruly, we threaten to bomb them. In everyday personal contacts, we often strive to control the behavior of others via censure, snubbing, disapproval, or banishment. Indeed, the extent to which punishment is used as a technique for behavior control seems to be limited only by the degree to which people can gain the necessary power to get away with it.

The point that needs emphasis is that all punishing is done with the intention of reducing the tendencies of another person to behave in a certain unwanted way. Certainly there is no gainsaying the possibility of discouraging someone from doing something by punishing or threatening him. The continued existence of murderers and mischievous little boys, however, seems somehow to suggest that punishment and its promise are distinctly less than sure-fire cures for undesirable behavior. Furthermore, many experiments, both with rats and with people, in laboratory settings and in real life, indicate that punishment does not in fact do what it is commonly supposed to do.

The tactic of threat and punishment rests on the implicit presumption (derived from a simplified popular psychology) that, if reward can build up incremental tendencies to behave in certain ways, then punishment, by a straightforward process of subtraction, can tear them down. However, as is often true of convenient beliefs, matters are not so deliciously simple. Behavior that is followed by a reward is likely to recur. That much is a well-established psychological fact. It is doubtful, however, that behavior followed by punishment will stop for long. To be sure, punishment typically has the easily observable immediate effect of reducing, or at least interrupting, a tendency to act in a given way. Giving Johnny one across the lips is likely to divert him from impudent commentaries; doing it regularly may well stop the impudent commentaries altogether. This result certainly is largely responsible for punishment's widespread use in the face of indications that its effects are often only temporary—that it does not actually eliminate behavior but accomplishes only an impermanent suppression of it. However, temporary suppression of noxious behavior may be sufficiently rewarding to the *user* of punishment to encourage him in its further use.

There may well be circumstances, of course, when temporary suppression is sufficient or maybe even essential. But this transitory effect is frequently obtained at tremendous cost in the form of reductions in the overall efficiency and happiness of people and groups and is likely to be detrimental to personnel identification with the system or its leaders or both. Punishment does not seem truly to reduce behavior tendencies. Also, unlike reward, it seems to work to the disadvantage of both the punished person *and* the punishing agent. The unpleasantness of the experience for the punished individual tends to generate strong emotions, including disruptive or disabling anxieties. This much may be obvious. Less obvious, though, is the fact that punishment tends to generate aversions, which lead to tendencies to escape from the punishment and/or to retaliate against its purveyors or their representatives. Neither of these predilections seems consonant with desires to foster attachment to the system or work-group solidarity.

The use of punishment, in fact, yields a whole array of unfortunate by-products. In addition to those already mentioned, its use tends to create a kind of conflict between the behavior that leads to punishment (for example, writing sloppy reports) and the behavior that can avoid punishment (writing neater, more thorough reports). It doesn't require a psychologist to know that a man cannot do both at once, but both tendencies may be generated within him. He had the disposition toward sloppy report writing to begin with—that's the reason for the punishment. Now his supervisor has generated a new disposition (writing more thorough reports) that can keep him from being chewed out. Behavior that will avoid punishment may alternate with previously punished behavior, sometimes in rapid oscillation, and both may blur finally into some uncoordinated, unproductive form of conduct. Such a conflict will be at its worst when an individual does not even perceive why he is being punished, is unaware of what he is expected to do instead, has little control over the situation, or feels the punishment to be unjust. He then will feel victimized and may very well develop deep, long-lasting grudges against the punishing agent and the system he represents.

It may seem obvious to a supervisor that a worker should be punished or reprimanded, but it is not always so obvious to the employee. He may see his performance as completely adequate. Even if he does see shortcomings in it, he may not see what he can do about it or even that it is his fault. He may simply feel, for one reason or another, that he lacks the ability to control it. Punishment doesn't help him. It doesn't give him any new ways to control or modify his behavior, it doesn't give him any real basis for developing needs that could be met by more acceptable levels of performance, and it certainly does nothing to cement the collaborative nature of the supervisory relationship. What it does tend to do is make him edgy, resentful, mistrustful, unhappy, and disposed to look elsewhere for employment.

In extreme cases, punishment or threat can induce serious fear and anxiety. The more the employee is accustomed to behaving in the undesirable manner and the more he feels the punishment to be unjust, the more likely he is to suffer severe emotional side effects as a result of punishment. Furthermore, it can happen under such circumstances that the desirable behavior that is intended to replace the punished behavior may quite literally act like an external physical restraint on the employee, generating opposition, rage, or frustration. Since frequently there is really no feasible escape from such a work situation short of resigning, the worker's condition may become chronic and actually result in various illnesses or otherwise interfere with the pursuits of his daily life, to say nothing of his job performance.

Thus punishment is unpleasant and freighted with unfortunate by-products. And if that is not enough, punishment also tends to be a generally inefficient technique for influencing and controlling behavior. In the first place, its efficacy in suppressing performance normally depends on the continued presence of the punishing agent. At minimum, it therefore requires costly expenditures of managerial time and energy in the more or less continuous and wasteful monitoring of subordinate behavior. In the second place, the disaffections and resentments it engenders mean that punishment cannot contribute constructively to the problem-solving process because it very likely serves to inhibit the free and timely flow of information on which effective problem-solving critically depends.

The Humanistic Conception of Management

In rebuttal of my thesis, it may be argued that oftentimes a man deserves punishment on moral grounds. This may be true; but does it seem appropriate for work supervisors to function as judges and executioners? Rather, it seems a more sensible and productive strategy for the supervisor to seek the elimination of undesired behavior by *replacing* it with desired patterns of performance, a process that depends on positive relationship building, rather than negative punitive methods. Furthermore, by following such a course, a manager may earn himself a bonus in the form of freedom from feelings of guilt.

Realism, of course, requires acknowledgment of the necessity for making use of threats and punishment sometimes. Emergencies do arise, and there are times when no other technique is available or feasible. My point is not to categorically proscribe the use of punishment but to encourage an appreciation of the undesirability of many of its consequences and the fallacy of founding managerial methods on its use.

Over the long term, as Galbraith suggests, a far more efficient system is one that encourages perceptions of mutual benefit such that employees are disposed to accept the organization's objectives as legitimate and consonant with their own. Striving for the one then amounts to striving for the other. Achievement of such a system, I submit, tends to be facilitated by humane employee-centered styles of leadership and retarded by punitive work-centered styles. Nor is this merely the prattle of tender-minded organizational do-gooders. In contrast with work- or job-centered supervision with its authoritarian-punitive flavorings, employee-centered supervision, grounded in humanistic, help-oriented precepts, commonly yields demonstrably higher productivity and worker satisfaction. My own experiences indicate that an employee-centered style of supervision contributes to work group solidarity, satisfaction, and freedom from tension. Furthermore, supervisors rated as employee-centered have tended more often than their work-centered counterparts to be judged effective by their own superiors. Thus, I concur with Likert (1961) when he concludes: "Supervisors with the best records of performance focus their primary attention on the human aspect of their subordinates' problems and on endeavoring to build effective work groups with high performance goals."*

Humane thoughts, benevolent attitudes, and avoidance of a destructively punitive style are good managerial starting points. However, forging "effective work groups with high performance goals" also requires an orientation toward subordinates different from the paternalistic, big-brother, do-gooder posture often confused with a genuine employee-centered style. Paternalism is inconsistent with the kind of mutual respect, understanding, and trust essential to the durable maintenance of highly productive work groups. What is required as a primary operational pathway to effective organizational performance is widespread influential participation in decision-making and goal-setting. The simple fact is that people will be considerably more disposed to accept goals and to work harder for their attainment when they have some power to influence the setting of those goals and the selection of procedures for their achievement. Furthermore, I believe that the average worker would *prefer* to be productive and to take satisfaction from competent performance and a job well done. Unfortunately, managers and supervisors too often incline to the view that these noble sentiments apply only to themselves. In one organization I studied, for example, management tended both to

---

* For a less sanguine estimate of the evidence on this and related points, see Perrow (1972), Chapter 3.

exaggerate their subordinates' concerns with security and promotion and to underestimate their aspirations for solidarity with their superiors and their desire to take pride in their work. In fact, everybody in that organization, without regard to rank, was seeking a chance to take pride in the performance of his work and to be a member of a productive harmonious organizational unit.

After all, every organization is a goal-seeking system concerned with its success in achieving its ends. An effective organization is one with widely shared goals, high performance standards, and the will and skill to achieve them. In an effective organization, "productivity" and "efficiency" are not dirty words to be uttered in hushed tones or disguised under euphemistic labels. On the contrary, they are directly pertinent to the fundamental goals of the system. For management to deny this relevance (or to seem to) is simply to appear lacking in candor or good sense. Discussion can and must go forth with regard to suitable standards and criteria of performance, but not in a fashion seeming to obscure actual interests. Instead discussions should be pointed toward attempts to illuminate the organization's goals and finding means to measure success in their achievement. Anything else defeats the objectives of effectiveness and, at the same time, fosters suspicion, mistrust, and disrespect within the system.

The Functions of Participation

Resistance to production standards arises primarily because of beliefs that the standards have been set to advance the interests of the top organization members rather than the workers who are expected to comply with them. Whether this is literally true or not is quite beside the point; people behave not in terms of what is but in terms of what they believe. When they are excluded from decision-making, they tend to believe the worst. In any event, most people find it hard to trust in the inherent beneficence and magnanimity of privileged decision-makers. Production, then, becomes an arena of contention and of political gamesmanship, not of joint goal-seeking.

Widespread influential participation by organization members in authentic decision systems—the ones where the real decisions are made—can be expected to improve the respectability of production viewed as the attainment of group goals. It can thereby contribute intellectually and motivationally to more effective organizational performance. With the planned recruitment and development of appropriate skills (both technical and managerial), organizational effectiveness can be expected to improve as the mathematical product of combinations of motivation and skill. That is to say that neither skill nor motivation alone is a sufficient condition for an effective organization. Each, however, is a necessary condition, and each multiplies the effects of the other. Skill without the will to apply it is useless; motivation without the skill to direct it is pointless.

Variance in goal definitions will cause both motivation and skill, and hence effectiveness, to fall below their maximum utilities. The reason for motivation and skill to go down is self-evident; effectiveness falls with them because skill is always relative to some task or goal. When goals are uncertain, the skills (and other resources) with which it is desirable to populate a performance system cannot be well-defined. The result is that an optimal mix can occur only by chance. The process of goal-setting, therefore, is a most critical organizational activity. But it is an activity that will benefit the system most when it is carried on participatively with full realization that organizations are human systems. Their business is work, but their actual operation depends on people, individual goals, and their interplay. A supervisor who had learned his lesson well put it succinctly when asked how he would characterize his job: "getting the work out by counseling with the men and evaluating their performance, because work gets out through people."

Individualized Supervision

Work motivation (and the ways it relates to varied job conditions) is extremely complex; the individual differences in its modes of manifestation are many. In a recent book, Ray C. Hackman (1969) documented these points and highlighted the crucial significance of individualized supervision to fully effective management. Hackman pointed out that managers have a responsibility to "acquire information on the motivational systems of the men [they manage and] must try to adapt the available [rewards] to the range of individual differences among the men [working for them] (p. 155). Relating the organization democratically to the needs and interests of individual members, therefore, is a major managerial mission and is the paramount concern of our concept of counseling.

THE MATTER OF SKILLS

Without intending in any way to detract from its fundamental importance, I have nevertheless suggested in the preceding passages that there is more to organizational success than powerful participation. Skill is a critical component of effective organizational performance. Neither skill nor participation is a substitute for the other; nor does the presence of one ensure the presence of the other. Both are essential to high-quality performance; moreover, the impact of each is probably maximized in the presence of the other. Skill, however, is variegated. There are all kinds of skills, and it isn't always easy to interrelate them. This is most particularly true of the two broad families of skills that are identifiable in complex work organizations: *technical* skills and *interpersonal* skills.

These two classes of skills relate and contribute respectively to the task and maintenance functions of the organization. They arise and differentiate because of the very nature of work organizations as task-oriented social systems. To maximize its effectiveness, an organization must have access not only to the skills and abilities required for performance of its work but also to those organizational, communications, and human-relations proficiencies essential to establishing a cohering social entity that is motivated to perform.

Technical skills tend to be widely distributed within the system. Interpersonal skills tend to be more concentrated within managerial subsystems. In the modern era, in fact, a major—possibly even *the* major—managerial requisite is possession of interpersonal skill.

Furthermore, whereas technical skills, if varied, tend to be particular to the work of specific organizations, interpersonal skills are more general and, within limits, are applicable to any organization. Managerial skills, therefore, to the extent that they are capable of equation with interpersonal skills, tend to be universal and highly portable.

COUNSELING AS AN INTERPERSONAL SKILL

This book, of course, centers on questions of interpersonal skill, specifically in the form of the counseling function. In subsequent chapters, I shall spell out more fully my concept of counseling. For now, it will suffice to explain it as involving a combination of attitudes and abilities especially germane to human social intercourse.

Counseling, as a set of managerial/supervisory functions, has come increasingly to be accepted as a component of management's panoply of skills. Focusing on motivational and communicative arts while implying concern and respect for individual differences, the counseling perspective is based on a primary impulse toward democratization of organizational life. Proficiency in implementing that perspective can contribute ingredients essential to the overall effectiveness of organizational enterprise.

References

Bennis, W. G., & Slater, P. E. *The temporary society.* New York: Harper & Row, 1968.

Blake, R. R., & Mouton, J. S. *Building a dynamic corporation through grid organization development.* Reading, Mass.: Addison-Wesley, 1969.

Galbraith, J. K. *The new industrial state.* Boston: Houghton Mifflin, 1967.

Hackman, R. *The motivated working adult.* New York: American Management Association, 1969.

Hollander, E. P., & Hunt, R. G. (Eds.) *Current perspectives in social psychology.* (3rd ed.) New York: Oxford, 1971.

Likert, R. *New patterns of management.* New York: McGraw-Hill, 1961.

Likert, R. *The human organization.* New York: McGraw-Hill, 1967.

March, J. G., & Simon, H. *Organizations.* New York: Wiley, 1958.

Perrow, C. *Complex organizations: A critical essay.* Glenview, Ill.: Scott, Foresman, 1972.

Rice, A. K. *The enterprise and its environment.* London: Tavistock Publications, 1963.

Recommended Readings

Dowling, W. F., Jr., & Sayles, L. R. *How managers motivate: The imperatives of supervision.* New York: McGraw-Hill, 1971. (A good all-around book that deals in practical terms with many management problems. Chapter 4 is a very helpful discussion of administering positive discipline.)

Gellerman, S. *Management by motivation.* New York: American Management Assn., 1968. (A well-known comprehensive treatment of motivational concepts and their application.)

Hunt, R. G. On the work itself. In E. J. Miller (Ed.), *Task and organization.* London: Tavistock Publications, in press. (Reviews the nature of tasks and the ways they limit management-decision alternatives.)

Maslow, A. H. *Eupsychian management.* Homewood, Ill.: Irwin-Dorsey, 1965. (A remarkable, stimulating, humanistic perspective on the issues of management.)

Seashore, S. E., Marrow, A. J., & Bowers, D. G. *Management by participation.* New York: Harper & Row, 1967. (A basic source on the subject.)

Skinner, B. F. *Beyond freedom and dignity.* New York: Knopf, 1972. (The great behaviorist reviews the essentials of "behavior technology," together with the fundamental social values at stake. The book includes extended discussion of punishment and other techniques for controlling behavior.)

Building
Effective
Organizations:
Organic System
Development

To its management, every organization presents two fundamental challenges: administration and development. Broadly speaking, administration is helping an organization follow established operating rules (including those related to problem-solving). It is an activity consonant with what I earlier called the "conservational dynamic" in organizations. Development, on the other hand, is change-oriented; it seeks to find better operating rules and so may (although it doesn't always) further the transformational thrust in organizations. This chapter deals expressly with the developmental challenge.

Around the general subject of organizational development (or OD, as the in-crowd calls it) have grown up various schools of thought, a considerable literature, something of a mystique, and assorted types of "true believers." I cannot review all of them here, but a few words are in order to at least establish my own general attitudes on the subject.

Effective Managers and Effective Organizations

Practical people are rightfully wary of terminological hair-splitting. Nevertheless, it is useful to distinguish between *organizational* and *managerial* development. Organizational development calls attention to the organization as a whole, with its many functioning parts and personnel. Managerial development focuses on only a subset of organization functions and usually on the people who perform them, rather than on the functions themselves. The former notion (OD) is thus considerably broader in its references than is managerial development. Managerial development is but one means to OD ends, albeit an especially important means.

Chapter 2 advertised the utility of system concepts of organization and presented the idea that organizational effectiveness is chiefly a matter of the quantity, quality, allocation, and use of various operationally relevant resources within a continuing system of purposeful activities. To make sound use of this idea and to appreciate the distinction between organizational and managerial development, we need to re-examine a theme first mentioned in Chapter 2: serious attempts to increase system effectiveness must begin with an orientation toward the organization as the primary target of development and not with an orientation toward the people who populate it.

To be sure, OD efforts will commonly require that attention be paid to people; the interests of people as human beings are natural things to stress when OD programs are structured. Procedurally, however, OD activities will more properly focus not on people *per se* but more precisely on selected characteristics that people may have (for example, skills, attitudes, and habits) *and* on the organizational structures that impede or facilitate desired performance outputs and employee satisfaction.

Yet, wittingly or unwittingly, managerial development has tended to become the major preoccupation of OD efforts. Despite rhetoric about holding system-wide perspectives that include structural considerations, an excessively large proportion of OD activity zeroes in on "people change" (whether the people to be changed are managers or others) to the virtual exclusion of anything else. Some experts seem to think (or act anyway) as if the sole useful model for OD is the clinical practice of diagnosing and treating the illnesses of individual sufferers and producing a paradise on earth in the process. For them, the basic question with which to begin seeking ways to initate and sustain developmental undertakings is: What's wrong with *you* (and there certainly must be something)?

Questions like that have their place in OD, but they are better nested in something that, to continue the medical metaphor, might be called a public-health model. Such a model highlights these questions: What's wrong with the *system*? Why does it work the way it does? What is necessary to change it? People (or, more exactly, their attributes), and particularly managers, will obviously come in for close consideration when answers to those questions are sought, but the system perspective of a public-health model implies several interesting possibilities:

1. Effective people, by themselves, do not necessarily make an effective organization.
2. An effective organization may sometimes be achieved without any *direct* efforts at changing individual people.
3. Trying to change organization members and/or their interpersonal relations may not always be the easiest, cheapest, wisest, or even a desirable approach to OD.
4. Things are always terribly complicated in organizations.

OD Defined

Comfort seems generally to be somehow found in pithy definitions, even when the thing defined often remains about as vague afterward as it was before. So what about OD? Well, definitions of it abound. Some are long, some are short. Richard Beckhard (1969) has succeeded in getting one into about as few words as anybody. He defines organizational development as any "planned organization-wide effort, managed from the top, to increase organization effectiveness and health through planned interventions in the organization's 'processes' using behavioral science knowledge" (p. 9).

Plainly this definition raises at least as many questions as it answers (and probably more), but it is representative and it serves as an introduction to what I shall be saying later in this chapter about phasing development efforts. Furthermore, Beckhard's inclusion of the term "health" in his definition is suggestive of the humanistic connotations that have accrued to the term "OD." But because of this suggestion, or because of my stress on interpersonal processes, or because so much writing on OD is people-change-centered or clinically flavored, the conclusion should not be drawn that disciplines such as operations research, systems analysis, critical-path analysis, cost/benefit studies, and the like are irrelevant to OD. They are highly relevant. Moreover, they are no less relevant than people-change methodologies. Indeed, since it is the organization that is being developed, the system-resource perspective on OD that I have urged makes just that point, implicitly perhaps, but nonetheless emphatically. The National Training Laboratory does not hold a patent on organizational development, and the T-group is not yet the royal road to organizational success.

For its benefits to exceed its costs, OD must be integrated around a systems-type attitude toward organization, a philosophy of management that points to basic system priorities, and a practicable interpersonal strategy for expressing that philosophy. Counseling and participative concepts are peculiarly appropriate ones around which to formulate administrative strategies. But they are also useful operational vehicles for synthesizing and carrying forward diversified OD undertakings.

Some Assumptions and Objectives for Organizational Development

Coherent implementation of the developmental function of management requires creation of a plan—a plan useful on a continuing basis but subject to progressive change. This plan should be explicitly oriented toward (1) identifying organization problems and goals for change, (2) producing methods for solutions to those problems, and (3) developing means for the agreeable assessment of goal achievement.

The approach I shall presently describe as a point of departure in these matters is founded on two broad assumptions, satisfaction of which is a prerequisite to its application:

1. There exists in the organization a general commitment to the objective of broadening the base of influential participation in problem-solving and decision-making within the system—a commitment to some form of authentic participative management. Further, a basic willingness on the part of top management to share power more widely and to encourage others to do likewise must be assumed.

Thus the assumption is that top management is prepared to accept, at least as a working principle, the substance of participation and not merely its forms. Both theoretically and factually, it seems evident that what counts is not the simple fact of participation but the *instrumental value* of participation in allowing people to influence decisions and thereby control their fate. In brief, participation is a means, not an end in itself.

2. The second assumption is that any development program must be consistent with development philosophies and structures

existing at top executive levels in the organization and in essential harmony with management formats throughout the system. Full management integration and support are taken for granted in my approach, the character of which is known in policy science circles as *devolutionary*. That is to say, it depends on a *voluntary* extension of the participative principle, in stages, from the top down to the working level.

PARTICIPATION AND DEVELOPMENT

Plainly, a participative direction is assumed to be an appropriate one in which to develop management systems. For one thing, it is consistent with general cultural predilections within a democratic society. For another, it is consistent with the increasing maturity, levels of personal responsibility and education, and motivational properties of the typical organization member. Furthermore, since social systems tend to maintain the status quo, participation can help diagnose those tendencies more quickly and so can serve as a hedge against backsliding in organizational change programs.

However, no specific management procedure or general mode of operation is likely to be congenial to everybody. Participative, group-based methodologies are no exception to this rule. Their success depends on the motivation of organization members to operate with them. In the short term, motivation will depend on perceptions of the likelihood that participation will yield some payoff. In the long term, continuity of motivation will depend on *actual* payoff; that is, participation must be shown to be in the interests of the participants. An organization will need to guarantee that in order to be successful at installing participative management. And, if payoff can be produced, some of the marginally motivated may eventually become "believers."

No matter what, there will always be some who, for any of a number of reasons, will not find the game a happy one. There is no universally applicable managerial strategy known to man nor any absolutely sure-fire technique. Participative methods are no exception to this rule. Some managers or supervisors may find it too difficult to share power with subordinates, and some subordinates may simply not be sufficiently committed to the organization to care. What is to be done in such cases is a matter for deliberation, of course, but before an organization proceeds with a participative program a sufficient base of motivation and aptitude *must be known to exist* if that program is to be feasible.

Even if motivation and aptitude are present, it may still be necessary to develop skills in participative techniques; any serious program will need to provide for that. I would also hope that programs can be devised with sufficient operational flexibility, at least at the working level, so as to be tolerant of diversity. If a worker does not or cannot participate, he may nevertheless be a valuable member of the system. Ideally, supervisors will be capable of making such judgments and of adapting their modes of supervision to such contingencies. Counseling training should help greatly in adapting working methods to individual idiosyncracies.

It is sufficient to justify participative strategies on moral-democratic grounds. However, participation happens to be defensible on organizational grounds, too. Partial and appropriate decentralization of control and decision systems works to enhance the quality of information pertinent to decisions. It encourages more timely decisions and decreases the load on communication channels. Broadened participation increases informational input and helps to improve upward and downward communication. It also results in surer problem identification and improves the aptness of solution as well as the level of commitment to organizational policies; it promotes a feeling of "we-ness." Furthermore, participative strategies address themselves expressly to what Frederick Herzberg (1959) called "motivational" factors in job performance. In other words, they help stimulate "an inner desire to make an effort" and do not rely entirely on extrinsic inducements such as money. Thus participative methodologies can be practical as well as desirable management strategies.

Organic Development

Organizational development efforts depend for effect basically on stimulating and channeling essentially natural organizational processes. What I have said about the organizational effects of participation underscores this organic proposition. Development must begin with the system as it is and encourage it to change itself in directions fundamentally consistent with its *existing* dispositions.

No manager or consultant can take a complex organization where it doesn't want to go. He can facilitate or impede organizational movement by a variety of means, including identification of motives, provision of policies, structures and technologies, training, information, coordination, and the like. In a limited way, he may also be able to "educate" the organization about directions it should "want" to take. Perhaps, too, as change occurs, other changes may be loosed that will include more suitable definitions of system goals. But the fact is that change and development are calculated to be gradual, fitful, agonizingly slow at times, and certainly piecemeal. Sensational results are the exception, not the rule. One must be wary of simplistic and excessive expectations for change in complex social systems.

Applying the Systems Perspective in Development

Organizational effectiveness has to do with how well a social system mobilizes resources to achieve its goals. But complex organizations have a multiplicity of goals, and they appear in different forms in different parts of the system. This not only makes it hard to define goals; it also makes it hard to know which resources are important. Hence a comprehensive development effort must be attentive to the entire complex of organizational goals. Difficult as this is; goals must be identified and formulated in ways meaningful to the levels and functions to which they relate.

As one moves closer to operational levels, goals become ever more specific, practical, occupational, and segmental. Executive-level organizational goals (or change targets) probably mean next to nothing to personnel at working levels. Top management's organizational goals are, in effect, quite general classification schemes serving to aggregate the many specific goals and subgoals operative at lower levels. Their purpose is to facilitate executive coordination, planning, and system-wide development. In a rational system, lower-level goals are higher-level subgoals; they represent instances of the general classification schemes defining goals at higher levels. It should always be possible to reconcile lower-level goals with higher-level goals. Such reconciliation, however, should be the task of higher and not lower management levels.

Having identified organizational goals, it is essential to develop some consensus about legitimate criteria for evaluating their achievement. Without such criteria, it is impossible to review and assess performance programs or to determine the effectiveness of proposals for change. A rational system must be evaluated, but in terms acceptable to its membership. Its management must also avoid becoming preoccupied with certain goals to the detriment of others.

THE SPECIAL PROBLEM OF PERFORMANCE REVIEWS

Productivity is an indispensable criterion for judging system effectiveness. Organizational provision for regular performance reviews at all system levels and for all system components is an obvious implication of this principle. However, in many circles, performance reviews have acquired a bad name. This tarnished reputation arises mostly from beliefs that performance reviews are necessarily harmful to the ego of the subordinate and, by setting the supervisor up as judge, put too much strain both on him and on his relationship with the subordinate. If these beliefs were valid, they would make a persuasive negative case, because their implication is that performance reviews are destructive of the very conditions essential to motivation and effective performance.

Yet feedback about performance seems to be fundamental to its control and improvement. Fitts and Posner (1967), for example, conclude from their studies of human performance that "feedback . . . can provide knowledge, motivation and reinforcement" (p. 28), all of which help to enhance the level of effort and quality of output. And Phillips and Wiener (1966), in their discussion of the application of cybernetic concepts to behavior change, give heavy emphasis to the role of feedback in controlling and sustaining system change. Moreover, most employees seem to want to know where they stand. (They do, after all, get repeated clues, not always consistent, from day-to-day interactions with their bosses.) Problems seem to arise chiefly when the performance review is conducted in narrow work, rather than broader employee-centered, frameworks (that is, when it fails to deal with the employee and his situation). Performance reviews will be problematic whenever they are purely evaluation-oriented (as distinct from development-oriented) and fail to seek ways of providing help to the employee or of establishing a mutual problem-solving attitude toward performance deficiencies. They will be problematic, too, whenever evaluation standards lack credibility to the employee and whenever the review fails to point clearly to realistic change targets and ways of achieving them. Summary statements in the order of "your performance is terrible, get it up by next week" don't help anybody very much. Goals, whether operational or developmental, need to be specific. So do the plans and criteria for their achievement. And all of these have to be meaningful to the people involved with them, a fact that argues powerfully for their collaborative elaboration.

A supervisor conducting a developmentally oriented performance review shows recognition for the strong points of performance and acknowledges his or her own responsibility for participating in an active search for ways of mutual problem-solving to strengthen performance. For example:

> Mary, your initiative has been outstanding and the accuracy of your work is exceptional. I'm really pleased with how you're doing. To be honest, though, I haven't been fully happy with certain of your work habits and I think maybe they've kept you from doing an even better job than you have. Let me tell you what I mean and you tell me what you think. Anyway let's look at what we've been doing on this job and see what ideas we can come up with . . .

In fact, performance reviews are not customarily conducted in brutally punitive ways; but reassuring as that may be, it still is true that they are usually conducted from an overly narrow evaluative stance, rather than from a broader developmental viewpoint. In a thoroughly sensible article published some time ago in the *Harvard Business Review* (1960), Harold Mayfield commented that a performance review "is simply an attempt to think clearly about each person's performance and future prospects against the background of his total work situation" (p. 82). When done in a framework of developmental objectives (individual as well as organizational), when integrated as an element in the development program, and when implemented in accord with the counseling perspective, there seems no inherent reason for the performance review to be regarded as a necessary evil to be tolerated and to be anticipated with dread and despair. Instead, a review can become a natural part of the developmental and supervisory routine, innocuous in itself, but contributing significantly to both short-term supervisory and longer-term developmental ends.

MORE ON THE SYSTEM VIEW OF GOAL ACHIEVEMENT

Obviously, it is impossible to sustain attention on all organizational goals simultaneously. People are people, not gods, even if some of them have trouble believing that and others are convinced that computers make the trip to Olympus a short one. What's more, interest in particular goals will vary depending on time and circumstances, as will willingness to sacrifice one goal for another. Yet it is desirable to provide some more or less formal means of monitoring goals on a system-wide basis so that an organization's aggregate level of effectiveness can be evaluated and bases can be determined for goal trade-off. In other words, I am proposing that organizational goals be defined as completely as possible and that methods be sought for keeping a continuing review of all of them, even though interest fastens on them selectively at different times. In such a situation, obviously, management-information systems and associated techniques (such as PERT and Planning/Programming/Budgeting) have great utility.

Most of the operational goals in organizations are apt to be quite mundane in comparison with the breathtakingly grand objectives often trumpeted at executive levels. Unfortunately, this fact sometimes leads to the neglect (benign or other) of working-level goals and to no more than lethargic quests for improved means for their specific achievement. Instead, totalistic and universalistic organizational panaceas are sought. There is much magical thinking among hard-nosed executives. But the intractable fact is that operational objectives define the real workings of the system. As someone has said, policy is procedure. There is no alternative to looking closely at working-level objectives. The truly astute manager will prepare for many nickel-and-dime development operations, of little import and drama in themselves, but aggregating to a more effective system.

Phasing Development Efforts

The devolutionary method of change depends upon a progressive process of generating goals, evaluations, change targets, and plans. It requires that attitudes toward change be worked through and that commitment to the participative process emerge. And, of course, it depends on development of viable participative mechanisms. This process needs to begin at the top and be substantially accomplished at each level before proceeding down to the next level.

When an organization is structured differently from what is typical (with very few hierarchical levels or in project form), a different procedure might be useful. But since bureaucratic structures are so widespread, I shall simply ignore other forms. Thus, in the usual case, I would envisage a partially phased introduction of participative programs, beginning at executive levels and working progressively downward to working levels or first-line supervision. At each level, following Likert's principle of the "linking-pin," at least one participant would connect the working group to another at another level, thus forming a steady line of communication and influence. (It is not necessarily a wholly reliable one, however, and we shall consider this problem shortly.) A phased approach to development is helpful as a way of breaking out from traditional bureaucratic molds of decision-making (even if bureaucratic appearances still remain). The approach provides for gradual change, with each change laying a foundation for the next. It allows experience and example to encourage managerial and supervisory personnel to risk sharing responsibility for decisions with their subordinates and to reassure superiors of the basic responsibility of their subordinates.

Phasing development efforts, like the concept of organic development, is a more or less direct extension of the system perspective on organization. By introducing change gradually and purposefully, opportunities for planning and thoughtful selection of change targets and tactics are increased. Furthermore, chances of detecting both signs and sources of resistance to change and unanticipated consequences are improved, as are prospects for finding timely solutions to them. Most importantly, phasing provides for the progressive development of structures and feedback loops that can support planning and change in successive organizational subsystems.

In addition, a phased developmental approach helps overcome a major barrier to authentic implementation of participative methods—that is, the fact that people do not view group discussions as part of their job. This perception largely rests on the fact that such group processes rarely have identifiable effects on the job. Instead, if real decisions are made by the group, one may reasonably expect these attitudes to change. Furthermore, since a mainly hierarchical organizational structure requires each group or level to depend for influence at the next level on its representative there, it is basic as a precondition to the success of the participative program that the representative at that level be perceived to be influential.

A STRUCTURE FOR A DEVELOPMENT PROGRAM

Phase I: In a comprehensive development program, the first essential ingredient is the structural and operational formalization of a top-level policy panel (or something similar). This is a prerequisite because such a structure must serve as a nucleus for operations within the system, operating both as the highest level in the interlinked policy-making system and as the primary coordinating unit for development efforts.

Because it is necessary at the outset to clarify top-management attitudes, beliefs, and concepts about possible directions for change and to determine appropriate general strategies for development, it will usually be advisable to set aside several early meetings of the executive policy panel expressly for detailed discussion of these matters. These discussions should include a level-by-level and unit-by-unit inventory, presented in the form of reports from appropriate unit heads, of existing practices concerning group meetings, delegations of authority, apparent impediments to delegation, and program planning at all organizational levels.

Before beginning any program of development and for sustaining it once it has begun, it is fundamental that objectives be clearly stated and that agreement be reached concerning means for indexing goal achievement. Since this is a demanding task requiring concentration, effort, and insulation from routine demands of work, it is commonly useful to provide for an off-site "kick-off" conference or retreat of the policy panel to consider these matters. This conference should be charged with responsibility for producing a searching and detailed statement of its conclusions—one that includes specification of organizational goals, broad change targets, and methods that will be used to measure their achievement. As a means for determining a solid point of departure and a frame of reference for managing development efforts, a careful inventory of the current availability of relevant information within the system and the determination of needs for additional information (along with methods for its attainment) will repay the effort.

Some such body as a policy panel must also exist to determine ways of monitoring performance within the organization and to provide regular, comprehensive performance reviews that will produce periodic evaluations of program achievements. Development targets can be amended on the basis of these evaluations and continuing consideration can be given to the revision of strategies and tactics for development.

Some high-level policy group must assume responsibility for regular review of development efforts, problems, and needs to ensure maintenance of development energy and timely identification and solution of impending difficulties. As Phillips and Wiener (1966) point out: "Systems must be worked at to be maintained" (p. 87). That is even truer of change.

Since training is an important component of any development effort, a training supervisor or specialist can be a useful addition to the staff. The training supervisor can be assigned to provide policy-makers with an inventory of formal and informal training programs and procedures being used in the organization. These may then be evaluated in relation to the organization's goals, and provisional training needs may be anticipated. One component of training-program reviews should be consideration of the kinds of training that can be provided locally and the kinds better centralized or contracted out and why. Training reviews should become a periodic, organizational policy-making activity.

The success of any comprehensive development effort (especially one premised on democratic principles) requires a general (if not total) openness of operation to allay suspicion and resistance to change. To that end, among other efforts, policy-makers might schedule meetings with the officers of the organization's union or employee association. The philosophy, goals, and evaluative criteria proposed by management can then be discussed in detail, and ways can be explored for union participation in management decisions. A good time for initiating these meetings would be immediately following any management retreat.

The generally hierarchical character of most organizational structures frequently results in a surprisingly long channel of communication from top to bottom—a channel replete with juncture points at which "noise" can occur. Grapevines aside, each man is dependent in greater or lesser degree on his immediate superior to transmit intelligence upward and downward. This is not a fully trustworthy system. Some redundancy would enhance its reliability, and it is also desirable to have alternative *cross-hierarchical* channels of communication. Organizational newsletters help with this, but such measures alone are too passive and formalistic and typically too one-sided as well. A more dynamic alternative is needed to provide upward as well as downward intelligence flow. A union can often serve this purpose well if relations between it and the system's policy-makers are somehow formalized and a pattern of regular meetings of the two is established. If no union or similar structure exists, some alternative vehicle will need to be found for this purpose. The same considerations apply to management. Some kind of all-management structure is needed to serve as a forum, to be an instrument for special-purpose programs, and to better integrate the management family. Organizationally sponsored management clubs can be helpful for these purposes, especially if they include all management and if their operations are closely coordinated with organizational policy-making. An important continuing function that a management club can serve is to remain attentive to the peculiarly difficult problem of keeping decision-making from being bucked up or down the management line. There is a persistent tendency in bureaucracies to defer decision to the next level and, when possible, to pass difficult decisions on to someone else. (There is in some quarters a pointed label for this practice: the protect-your-arse syndrome). For decentralized decision-making to work and for participation to be meaningful, control of this tendency is imperative. Informal pressures that can generate from discussions in work groups and management clubs can help.

Of course, there is no way to guarantee the effectiveness of any technique, including the ones mentioned here. They are certainly not exhaustive, and they should be looked on as tentative, general orientations. They should not be treated as rules nor be implemented ritualistically. Flexibility of operation should be the keynote. Policy-making subsystems and all subordinate structures should be encouraged, consistent with strategic policies, to develop their own operating procedures and to pursue innovative programs.

In all of this, top management has an overriding responsibility to foster the necessary atmosphere and support while keeping an eye on overall program objectives. Tolerance is essential to discipline, as is a keen understanding that much of the learning that will need to take place during earlier portions of any developmental program centers around discovering exactly what policy decisions really are, how they can be made, and what kinds can realistically be made at different system levels. Consistent task orientation and productive problem-solving throughout the organization are not likely to emerge until development is rather far along the road.

Phase II: This second phase is essentially preparatory for further activities. It actually is an extension of Phase I and is likely to overlap with it in time. Consisting mainly of orientation toward and enhancement of proficiency in the philosophies and methods of management that inform the organization and describe its supervisory goals, Phase II serves to point directions, crystallize motivations, clarify expectations, and initiate participative problem-solving. *Counseling training*, as we shall see, is expressly designed to serve these ends. Indeed, initiation of such training might be a central feature of Phase II operations. For all these reasons, Phase II emphases begin quite naturally to gravitate toward the working level and the first line of supervision.

At best, formal counseling training only begins a process. Like that of many other more particular OD methods, its impact depends on follow-on activities. These will usually take one or both of two general forms: (a) skill-development workshops and (b) means for identifying barriers to skill implementation. Given the larger nature of most OD programs, these objectives will probably be best accomplished by arranging next-higher-level meetings for first-line supervisors for the purpose of discussing experiences, problems, and other issues connected with counseling and for seeking means to sharpen interpersonal skills further. These meetings can constitute an initiation of participative sessions that can be regularized and extended during Phase III. If desired, consideration of group methods of supervision could be initiated during these counseling-oriented workshops. Identification of barriers to the implementation of counseling would now, along with other organizational issues, be an integral part of the interlinked participatory problem-solving network. No separate mechanisms would be necessary.

Implementation of Phase I proposals by organizational policy-makers will soon necessitate parallel activities at middle-management levels. To facilitate this process up and down the line, middle managers would be encouraged to initiate regular goal-setting, program planning, problem-solving and performance-review meetings with subordinate management personnel. Any special problems with the implementation of this practice in particular organizations should be priority subjects for discussion in policy groups.

During this second phase of developmental operations, consideration should be given to providing suitable skills training in order to prepare supervisory and management personnel for the effective conduct of group meetings. Training programs in conference leadership and group-discussion techniques that emphasize action orientation and generation of group decisions might profitably be placed on the OD agenda. In these training sessions, the idea of goal-directed group problem-solving should be stressed in addition to methods of eliciting group catharsis (although such methods may have a place in the overall scheme of things).

Phase III: The primary objective in this OD phase is regularization of lower-middle-level participative programs, the groundwork for which was laid during Phase II. Attention can begin to concentrate on the inauguration and consolidation of goal-setting, program planning, problem-solving, and performance-evaluation meetings at the next management level above the first line.

These could and probably should develop gradually out of previous supervisory counseling workshops. Timing and modes of initiation can be matters of judgment on the part of the organization's executives in consultation with middle management, but specific procedures should not be rigidly prescribed by these bodies. Careful attention will need to be given during this phase to the development of means for resolving the difficult problem of relating any personnel in small organizationally detached or remote posts-of-duty to the overall organizational program.

Phase IV: In effect, this phase is the climax of a development program. It consists entirely of the program's formal extension to the working level by the introduction of participative decision-making meetings there. During this period, it is important that first-line supervisors maintain perspective on the functions of the participative process and not lose sight of the fundamental desirability of maintaining flexibility and individuality in supervisory practice. To assist in this process, some time in lower middle-management-level meetings and in the management club (if one exists) could be given to consideration of the problems of motivating participation, the question of the nonparticipating employee and what to do about him, the desirability of adapting supervision to characteristics of individual employees, and similar matters.

Phase V: This is the period of evaluation; ideally it should take two and in certain cases three essential forms:

1. After a sufficient period of experience with Phase IV activities, a series of sessions at all managerial levels (and in the management club) and in meetings with the union should be devoted to judgmental evaluation of the experience. These

workshops should point toward a careful critique of practices and policies and culminate in *specific* proposals for changes to be implemented during Phase VI.

In addition to this generalized, subjective appraisal, another more objective one might well be conducted this way:

2. In the light of the performance goals and change targets set at each level of the system, careful and systematic reviews should be conducted in relation. to the criteria previously determined to be suitable. This penultimate review should obviously not preclude earlier performance evaluations if they are desired (and often they will be).

Finally, when the program is in fact a pilot program, more searching evaluation is in order prior to its organizational installation. Therefore:

3. Provision should be made for the collection, perhaps by consultants, of hard data useful for evaluation and description of the OD program's characteristics. (Methods for accomplishing this can include some kinds of pre-post measurement, so-called process evaluations, or both.)

Phase VI: This phase amounts to a consolidation of the essentials of the OD program as a continuing fact of organizational life. It should take into account changes proposed and agreed on in Phase V regarding policies and methods of management, and it should include provision for a regular policy-based recycling of program review and modification, perhaps annually.

This phase can also be the occasion for a full formal report of the activities, experiences, and outcomes of the program. During Phase VI it would be appropriate to offer a comprehensive evaluative report, with recommendations of all aspects of the program to top management. For best results, any such report, before delivery, should probably be submitted for commentary *throughout the system* and should include such commentary *unedited.* (The assumption is that top management is interested in facts and not merely acclaim.)

Summarized in outline, the essential features of the phased development program I have discussed are as follows:

OPERATIONS	OBSERVATIONS
Phase 0	
1. Conduct organization surveys.	Provide base-line data for evaluation.
Phase I	
1. Form executive panel, which may include consultants.	Coordinate program efforts with this policy body. Assure regular review of progress. Emphasize styles of and attitudes about management. Assure continuing feedback to panel.
2. Review change concepts, directions, methods. Conduct unit-by-unit inventory of existing practices and availability of information.	
3. Hold off-site retreat.	Operationalize change goals, targets, and criteria.
4. Review training needs and plan programs.	Bring in a training specialist if necessary.
5. Arrange meetings of panel with union. Regularize relations.	Review program goals and concepts. Encourage union participation in planning and decisions.
6. Form all-management club.	Use club as an additional two-way communication channel and an informal program-review body.
Phase II	
1. Institute counseling training.	Include all supervisory personnel.
2. Begin counseling follow-on programs such as skill workshops.	Orient training to working level.
3. Search for barriers to implementation of training. Plan methods of coping.	
4. Begin management training in ways of facilitating participation and group techniques (conference leadership and so on).	
5. Begin program of general meetings of first-line supervisors with immediate superiors.	Initiate participative practices, group problem-solving, and training-and-development troubleshooting. Get general management support.
6. Extend Phase I model to middle management. Have a formal liaison with executive panel.	Hold regular goal-setting and policy-planning meetings among and between middle managers and immediate subordinates.
Phase III	
1. Extend model to lower-middle-management level by regularizing meetings of first-line supervisors with superiors.	Prepare for including all personnel during next phase.
Phase IV	
1. Extend model to working level.	Continue to work on developing methods for motivating participation and for individualizing supervision.

OPERATIONS *(cont.)*	OBSERVATIONS *(cont.)*

Phase V

1. Evaluate the program.

Phase VI

Consider using a third party for objectivity.

1. Analyze, report, and review results of evaluation.
2. Institutionalize viable portions of program.
3. Scan system for new development needs.

Possibly seek revisions and begin new development cycle.

TIMING INNOVATIONS

To attach a development program of the type sketched here rigidly to a clock or calendar is impossible. Precisely what events will occur and when is uncertain and susceptible only to the grossest planning. Furthermore, the introduction of innovations will depend on the emergence of subsystem receptivity and judgments as to readiness. Haste and arbitrary procedures are to be avoided. As a rule of thumb, however, when starting from zero, an 18-month to 2-year period would be a reasonable interval to provide for the accomplishment of the kinds of things I have described.

CONSULTANT INVOLVEMENT

I have stressed the idea of organic development. Outside experts can nevertheless often help that process in a variety of ways. In addition to the perspective afforded by not being a regular member of the system, consultants can:

1. Bring to the organization theoretical, empirical, and procedural knowledge not otherwise available, thereby helping to enhance in-house capabilities.
2. Assist in the process of training and in defining training needs and methods.
3. Serve as participant observers, helping to manage, sustain, and identify barriers to the development process.
4. Provide evaluative services.
5. Maintain liaison with appropriate organizational departments and participate in planning-program applications.

Specific consultant services that might be envisaged for an OD project such as that sketched above might include, for example, program planning (including evaluations of applicability elsewhere in the organizational system), preparing and training instructors for counseling training, preparing and conducting off-site conferences, conducting counseling follow-on workshops, meeting as a resource-person with a policy panel, union, and/or management club, conducting review sessions and preparing and making reports, meeting with the management groups below the policy panel-level, and generally advising and maintaining liaisons with the organization's training personnel and other pertinent staff.

IN-HOUSE CAPABILITY

The strategy of developing and using in-house training resources is obviously defensible. However, it requires some tempering with careful evaluation of available resources in order to maximize or optimize the utility of their application. Although programs (especially those focusing on interpersonal skills) frequently run smoothly and generate favorable comment from participants, it has been my experience that certain deficiencies are commonplace in the implementation of those programs—deficiencies traceable to limitations in the capabilities of training personnel and their preparation for the conduct of the program.

Basically, these limitations center on two matters:

1. Appreciation of and readiness to follow a training *plan*. Too often, training-program events are treated as discrete and independent of one another, instead of as cumulative and interdependent. As a result, the thrust of training is blunted, and its impact is attenuated. Moreover, programs rooted in group-discussion techniques often have a seriously counterproductive tendency to treat discussion as good for its own sake rather than as a means to a training goal, achievement of which requires careful maintenance of focus in the program.
2. Insufficient development of the training skills of training personnel in organizations is distressingly normal. No training program can be any better than the technical skill with which it is implemented. When important limitations can be found in the skills presently available to an organization, training efforts are likely to be less than they could be.

Thus, before electing to undertake an OD program, in-house resources need careful appraisal, and a mix of consultant and in-house inputs should be chosen in the light of that evaluation. Frequently, consultant contributions will most profitably be directed to the planning of programs and the preparation of personnel rather than to routine program execution. And, too, consultant involvement in program implementation might be planned to provide systematic critique of instructional or other program formats and performance. In other words, consultant inputs to development should include augmentation of the system's *own* developmental capabilities. Except on the basis of a deliberate cost-effectiveness choice, an organization should not have to use a consultant for the same thing more than once or twice.

The Counseling Perspective and Organizational Development

I have described a managerial approach to organizational development. It stressed strategies and targets rather than specific tactics because it was premised on the belief that such tactics, in order to be maximally effective, must evolve organically from within the particular system itself. Specific development goals and concrete means for their prospective achievement must emerge from natural organizational processes and in forms pointedly meaningful within the organizational families to which they apply. An effective development program should generate its own specific activities. I have tried to make clear that a successful organization operates with policies and procedures adapted to its special characteristics. Therefore any major development program must itself reflect these realities. A managerially contrived development strategy can surely help to channel and stimulate innovative processes by providing, as and when required, appropriate policies, skills, structures, and supporting attitudes. However, it cannot hope to substitute for them or to by-pass intrinsic organizational dispositions.

Organizational development cannot be premised on monolithic methodologies. Ideally, developmental efforts should be multifaceted and technically differentiated across organization levels and functions. Whatever their scope, developmental efforts must be viewed from an evaluative stance; specific organizational activities must be seen in perspective of their objectives, limitations, and relations with other activities, and we must search for their larger implications and potential for further development.

As a managerial responsibility, organizational development requires thoughtful integration of a range of special-purpose activities. It presupposes dispositions toward change in the system but depends for success on planning and designing clear, cogent, and purposeful programs and on their skillful implementation. In the final analysis, development programs rely for impact on changes in organization policy and structure. Therefore, the development program itself must include means to accomplish such changes.

Thus, in addition to recommending the introduction of interpersonal counseling skills into supervisory roles, I have been emphasizing that their introduction will gain in effect if done according to a sensible plan. In addition, the overall impact from their introduction will be increased by embedding them in broader organization development programs. Conveniently, the counseling concept itself is quite well-adapted to serving as the nucleus and basic integrative principle for formulating organizational development plans and procedures. As an operational orientation toward supervision (at any level), use of the counseling *perspective* makes the intermeshing of all components of organizational functioning possible, thereby synthesizing and translating them into action within the critical supervisory relation. Counseling concepts and their associated interpersonal skills make it possible to pull together diverse inputs to the system. What is more, by facilitating both upward and downward communication, counseling practices in supervisory relations can help greatly in guaranteeing the feedback necessary to guide and control general system development. Thus counseling can be both a goal and an instrument of development within a participatory democratic framework.

References

Beckhard, R. *Organization development: Strategies and models.* Reading, Mass.: Addison-Wesley, 1969.

Davis, S. A. An organic problem-solving method of organizational change. *Journal of Applied Behavioral Science,* 1967, **3**.

Fitts, P. M., & Posner, M. I. *Human performance.* Monterey, Calif.: Brooks/Cole, 1967.

Herzberg, F., et al. *Motivation to work.* (2nd ed.) New York: Wiley, 1959.

Mayfield, H. In defense of performance appraisal. *Harvard Business Review,* March/April 1960, **38** (2), 81–87.

Phillips, E. L., & Wiener, D. N. *Short-term psychotherapy and structured behavior change.* New York: McGraw-Hill, 1966.

Recommended Readings

Clelland, D. I., & King, W. R. *Systems analysis and project management.* New York: McGraw-Hill, 1968. (Useful on the subject of project management as well as systems analysis.)

Dowling, W. F., Jr., & Sayles, L. R. *How managers motivate: The imperatives of supervision.* New York: McGraw-Hill, 1971. (Contains a useful section on project management as a new organizational role.)

Fordyce, J. K., & Weil, R. *Managing with people: A manager's handbook of organization development methods.* Reading, Mass.: Addison-Wesley, 1971. (A comprehensive how-to-do-it source book.)

Herzberg, F. *Work and the nature of man.* Cleveland: World, 1966. (A basic statement of "two-factor theories" of work motivation; to be read together with R. Hackman's book *The motivated working adult* [see Chapter 3] and V. Vroom's *Work and motivation,* New York: Wiley, 1964.)

Journal of Contemporary Business. Summer 1972. (A special issue devoted to organization development, but also useful as regards project management models.)

Schein, E., Bennis, W., & Beckhard, R. (Eds.) *Organization development.* Reading, Mass.: Addison-Wesley, 1969. (A series of six short paperbacks covering various aspects of OD, written by the editors or by such specialists as Blake and Mouton, Richard Walton, Paul Lawrence, and Jay Lorsch.)

Schmidt, W. H. *Organizational frontiers and human values.* Belmont, Calif.: Wadsworth, 1970. (A symposium by and for organizational students and leaders that confronts broad issues of change, technology, and social norms.)

chapter
five

The Counseling
Concept in a
Work Setting

Not long ago I asked the members of one large organization, managers and workers alike, what the word "counseling" meant to them. I also asked what they thought about its uses in the work setting. Nearly all the people I talked to thought it quite proper and desirable for work supervisors to counsel their subordinates, at least with regard to matters relevant to their work. Almost to a man, supervisors asserted that they already customarily counseled their subordinates, and the latter generally agreed with them. However, it seemed clear from our discussions that "what passes for counseling in the supervisory relation . . . would, in most cases, probably not be recognizable as such to a professional counselor" (Hunt & Lichtman, 1969). Allowing for some differences in emphasis, counseling was basically conceived as a process of giving advice and controlling performance in a friendly and helpful way.

In effect, it seemed to me that counseling had simply been assimilated to a somewhat "softened" but still paternalistic version of the classical bureaucratic authority-based definition of superior-subordinate relations. This version was epitomized by one first-line supervisor, who, when asked what he thought counseling was, replied "well, it's certainly related to a man's work; it's a means of giving advice, directives, or suggestions." Such an imperfect, essentially foreshortened comprehension of the counseling perspective is undoubtedly more the rule than the exception in managerial circles. A gross attenuation of counseling's utilities and a perpetuation of traditional supervisory practices can only result from it. In addition, managers, perceiving nothing really new or different about "counseling," are apt rather innocently to exaggerate their capabilities as counselors. The fact is that effective counseling, like most other managerial functions, requires interpersonal skills that can commonly be acquired with opportunity and application. Reasonable understanding of the counseling concept is a necessary preliminary to the development of such skill and its fruitful application.

Counseling Defined

As I see it, counseling involves a combination of attitudes and abilities that have special relevance to the processes of human social intercourse. It entails a focusing of managerial attention on processes of human motivation and interpersonal communication and implies concern and respect for individual differences along with the democratization of organizational life. Therefore, counseling is both an expression of and a means for achieving the goals of an employee-centered orientation toward management, which, as Rensis Likert observed, necessarily implies extensive use of individual coaching and counseling.

Unfortunately, there is no simple explicit definition of counseling that can do full justice to the many varied forms and settings in which it is practiced. What definitions exist are either very broad and general* or particular to some specific type or target of counseling (for example, vocational counseling, pastoral counseling, or marriage counseling). However, a generally serviceable inclusive definition (a characterization, really) might run something like this: *counseling is a problem-focused interaction process. Its object is learning, growth, and changed behavior. It is facilitated by the counselor's conveying genuine feelings of warmth and spontaneity, tolerance, respect, and sincerity.*

This concept of counseling emphasizes the development of help-oriented interpersonal relations as effective problem-solving vehicles premised on individual understanding and high levels of mutual trust. It directs attention to behavior rather than to the "inner dynamics" of the person. In other words, the concept I am presenting is

---

*Krumboltz (1970), for instance, has said, "Counseling consists of whatever ethical activities a counselor undertakes in an effort to help the client engage in those types of behavior which will lead to a resolution of the client's problems."

in keeping with what has been called a behavioral and developmental approach to counseling (see Osipow & Walsh, 1970, especially Chapter 1). Similar to the example of S. W. Bijou (1966), this concept charges the counselor with first seeking direct modification of behavior by arriving at an appreciation of the factors supporting that behavior, next devising a program for learning more effective ways of acting, and then arranging conditions that will facilitate that learning. Interestingly, these ideas are echoed in much modern management writing, and they obviously harmonize with concepts of the developmental responsibilities of managers. This approach resonates, too, with contemporary prescriptions regarding performance control and work incentives (see, for instance, Dowling & Sayles, 1971, Chapter 5).

To assure achievement of its goals, counseling requires an awareness of communication dynamics and a preparedness to face and deal with emotions. Furthermore, modern thinking about counseling centers on an idea of reciprocal give-and-take as a means of mutual problem-solving. It will vary in details of method, depending on problems and purposes, but counseling will always retain an essentially interpersonal quality.

Counseling in the Supervisory Relation

Much (although not all) of the development and refinement of counseling concepts has taken place in clinical or quasi-clinical contexts. But plainly, we cannot seriously entertain the notion of developing managers and work supervisors as clinicians. Indeed, it would probably not be desirable even if we could, for there are fundamental differences between the usual clinical relationship and its work counterpart.

Nevertheless, even if the intention is not to train supervisors as clinical specialists, it can still be useful to scrutinize the counseling concept and perspective for its general relevance to work management and for its potential for procedural adaptation to the supervisory setting. Although it may seem to be making a virtue of necessity, in actuality the fact that prevailing conceptions of counseling are loosely drawn is something of an advantage. For instance, it permits us to shape them to the particular needs and realities of the work setting without injury to their essential meaning.

The Rationale for Supervisory Counseling

Interest in applying counseling methods in the work context is not wholly new. More than a few organizations have maintained some kind of counseling service as a psychological and social device for helping employees cope with organizational and personal problems, usually on the assumption that unsolved individual problems may spill over to degrade work performance or the work environment. The classic Western Electric researchers* in the late '20s and early '30s directed attention to the idea of enhancing organizational life by providing counseling to workers by vividly illuminating the enormous influence of work groups and the attitudes of their members in determining the structure and operational character of organizations. However, the counseling idea never really caught fire, possibly because in practice it entailed the expendable luxury of importing into the enterprise professional counselors or personnel specialists who lacked identification with and relevance to the "nitty-gritty" features of the job. Furthermore, the image and thrust of counseling in these professional hands probably tend to become too much centered on individuals and personalities, rather than on organizations and job performance.

At any rate, until recently, little widespread enthusiasm had germinated for the routine use of counseling in work organizations. My hope now is to give new impetus to the counseling function by relating it clearly to the concepts of management I have sketched in the previous chapters, by identifying it directly with supervisory functions, and by reorienting the counseling concept to give it less the flavoring of personal therapy. According to these precepts, *counseling is an integral managerial function*, expressing an approach to supervision that permits a quite particular understanding of the manager's role to be put into action.

This understanding is by no means necessarily alien to the mental-health concerns of earlier (and some contemporary) advocates of industrial counseling. Indeed, I have tried to stress that it is very

---

*The research carried out at the Hawthorne, Illinois, plant of the Western Electric Company, with Elton Mayo as research director, put heavy emphasis on the informal organization. Human relations in industry and the human-relations school of organizational thought became significant social and intellectual developments in the wake of these studies. For descriptions, discussion, and critique of these studies, see Homans (1950), Roethlisberger and Dickson (1939), and Perrow (1972).

much rooted in traditions of concern for the humanization of organizations and for the reduction of tensions in the work environment. However, it is also an understanding built on a desire to foster high performance standards as well as high morale. The counseling proposal, in brief, is that productive organizations can be pleasant organizations. Basically, what it takes to accomplish these dual objectives is the use of a style of organizational leadership pivoting on concern for the needs and interests of individual workers and a leadership strategy directed toward fostering the development of cohesive work groups.

The reappraisal of managerial functions awakened by more recent organizational theories has resulted in the redefinition and enlargement of managerial roles. To deal effectively with the interpersonal unit that is basic to employee-centered managerial orientations, the modern supervisor needs to develop a repertoire of technical human-relations skills (described more fully in the next chapter). In other words, the counseling concept, as applied to the work context, is a sort of general rubric summarizing a complex of attitudes, interests, and skills that collectively define a fundamentally employee-centered approach to management. Recognizing the breadth of meaning involved, one can say that a requisite to fully effective management and leadership of people is the ability to form and implement a counseling relationship.

Counseling and the Supervisory Task

The modern supervisor-manager thus faces a demanding task. He must develop a highly varied and differentiated armamentarium of leadership skills, an acute sensitivity to problem identification, an ability to relate his skills appropriately to the problems confronted, and a generally artful and humane mode of implementing his responsibilities. Furthermore, the range of problems with which the organizational leader may be expected to cope is apt to extend beyond the narrow confines of the job to include subordinates' hopes, aspirations, frustrations, and the like. With special reference to counseling, therefore, it is crucial that supervisors learn where, when, and how to draw the limits of legitimate problems so as to avoid the unwitting and consuming practice of implicit psychiatry.

What, then, are the boundaries of employee counseling? Even when construed as broadly as I have here, the counseling function is by no means limitless. Guidelines need to be set so that supervisors can begin acquiring the necessary skills. Unless the counseling function is properly bounded, it is difficult to imagine it becoming an effectively performed, routine supervisory function—difficult to imagine, that is, unless we are prepared to equate counseling and supervision. Counseling is but *one* supervisory function, although one intimately interlinked with and affecting all the others. Supervisors may counsel, but they also organize work, evaluate performance, function in the communication system of the organization, and do many other things. In other words, counseling may be looked on as a component (albeit an especially important, central, and fundamental component) of the total supervisory role. Its effective performance requires particular skills and attitudes (trainable skills) at least partly different from those involved in other supervisory part-functions.

Obviously, there is a sense in which the counseling concept is integral to *all* supervisory functions; its perspectives pervade all supervisory activities. And counseling, as I stated earlier, is tantamount to an *approach* to real-time system management. In any case, specification of counseling skills depends on delimitation of the function to be performed.

The Two Points of Reference in Employee Counseling

W. J. Dickson and F. J. Roethlisberger (1966), two pioneers in the field of employee counseling, have appropriately observed that the currency of counseling has two sides: what a worker wants from his job and his life and what the organization wants of the worker. On the one hand, in varying measure, workers want such things as a steady, secure job, satisfying relations with fellow workers and supervisors, a sense of belonging and identity, recognition and equitable compensation, freedom from exploitation, and a chance to express and develop skills, just to name some of the possibilities. The organization, on the other hand, expects the worker to work hard, to meet standards efficiently, to observe rules of conduct on (and perhaps off) the job, to be willing to see management's side of things, to be responsible and mature, to be cooperative, and, above all, to be loyal. Needs and occasions for counseling generate from the abrasions caused by conflict among these wants or failures to satisfy them. For instance, in a 1953–54 study of job counseling at the Hawthorne plant of the Western Electric Company, Dickson found the most frequent problems of the 736 people counseled (in this case, by a professional counselor) to be:

Disturbances in outside relations (with spouses, in-laws, or neighbors).
Dissatisfaction with job or salary.
Demotion and downgrading (loss of status, reduction in pay, and so on).
Disappointment or frustration over lack of advancement in the firm.
Illness or health concerns.
Disturbances or breakdowns in relations with coworkers.
Disturbances or breakdowns in relations with supervisors.
Employee failure to measure up to company requirements (attendance, efficiency, and so on).
General personality disturbances (moodiness, alcoholism, irresponsible attitudes, and so on).

Especially noteworthy about Dickson's list (which, by the way, experience indicates to be about as representative today as it was in the '50s) is the fact that off-the-job problems head it. It also shows clearly how regularly counseling must involve encounters with personal matters. When one thinks of work supervisors in counseling relations with employees, therefore, it is both fair and necessary to ask whose agent the supervisor is. The psychiatrist or psychologist counseling a patient in a clinic or consulting room (except under special circumstances) is unambiguously the agent of the patient. His primary if not exclusive concern is the welfare and interests of his patient. The relationship is personal and almost categorically confidential. There normally is little confusion over where the counselor's responsibilities lie.

Generally the same things may be said of relations between attorneys and their clients and clergymen and their parishioners. But to say the same things of counseling relations between employees and their supervisors would be glib and misleading. As a counselor, the supervisor's image is mixed. He is simultaneously a member of two "families." He has an individual relationship with the particular employee, but he also has a relationship with and a responsibility to the organization. The employee-counseling relation articulates the organization and its needs and interests as well as the individual employee and his needs and interests. It reflects simultaneously an active concern on the part of the supervisor for the welfare of the organization and a commitment to the welfare of the human beings in it. Indeed, more than anything else, perhaps, the counseling relationship between supervisor and employee is expressive of modern managerial attempts to meld organizational and individual interests in an employee-centered organizational design.

The fact remains, however, that the individual and the organization are separate. Moreover, it follows from our construction of counseling as a *supervisory* function that the supervisor-counselor, by virtue of his position and role, will remain first and primarily an agent of the organization. That this fact will sometimes make employee counseling difficult or impossible cannot be denied. But nothing is gained by pretending that the supervisory counselor can consistently be the unambiguous agent of the employee. Indeed, such pretense can only subvert the basic honesty essential to establishing relations within which serious counseling can occur.

Given the role of the supervisor as primarily an agent of the organization and only secondarily an agent of the individual employee, one might be moved to wonder how a meaningful counseling relationship could ever really be established. That it is difficult I have acknowledged. What it comes to is a challenge to individual supervisors and to general enterprise management to authenticate their generalized employee-centered sentiments and then to create an organizational climate that can make possible the candor and commitment fundamental to genuine counseling. We shall return to this subject in the next chapter.

The Problem Focus of Employee Counseling

There seem to be two rather dissimilar counseling traditions. One of them can be roughly called person-focused and the other problem-focused. Although it is something of an oversimplification, one can say that person-focused counseling concentrates on the *person* and his characteristics. Problems are looked on as derivative. The purpose of this type of counseling is to change the person (or his attitudes or personality); the person's problems will then mostly take care of themselves.

On the other hand, the problem-focused tradition holds that there is no certainty that changing the person will eliminate his problems, especially if it should happen that his problems are not wholly derivative. More importantly, however, this tradition works with the idea that many human problems can be dealt with in their own right at their own level and that it is an error to complicate unnecessarily and prolong counseling by working on the person rather than on his problems. Even when the problems at issue are personal, a problem-focused approach is possible. Under such conditions, counseling is limited to the resolution of the particular problem and not to undertaking an overhaul of the total personality.

These approaches may each be useful for different purposes. But it is hard to imagine how employee counseling could be cast in anything other than a problem-focused framework. The supervisor lacks the time, the facilities, the skills, and hopefully the interest to become enmeshed in so demanding and consuming a task as general personal renovation. It is not his job to change employees. It *is* his job to solve problems related to his functions in the organizational system. Admittedly, solving problems will sometimes entail changing the employee's behavior. But it is a vital matter of emphasis. It seems inappropriate to focus employee counseling on the person of the employee. In the interest of both efficiency and effectiveness, its focus should be frankly on problems (including appropriate behavior). You may still ask, of course, which problems?

The answer to this question seems straightforward, but unfortunately it is easy to be glib about it. Supervisors should counsel employees about job-related problems. Problems not related to the job are not suitable objects for employee counseling, except incidentally. All this is easy to say, of course, but the rub is how to differentiate job-related from non-job-related problems (recall, for example, the contents of Dickson's list). There is no simple, pat answer to this question, and a multitude of "gray areas" exist that a moment's reflection will reveal. These judgments finally depend on the good sense and sound judgment of individual supervisors.

Supervisors can, however, be trained to become better at the job, and they can be selected with apt criteria in mind. Most importantly, supervisors can be supervised. What is needed is a layering of the supervisory counseling operations of organizations. The supervisor must have someone to whom he can turn for support and counsel—someone responsible for monitoring and developing his skills. In addition, arrangements can be made for group staff meetings at which problems can be discussed and courses of action evaluated. These are among the reasons for integrating counseling-skills development into larger-phased organization-development efforts after the fashion discussed in Chapter 4. Other possibilities (some of which are discussed in later chapters) doubtless exist. However, the point to be made is that organizational supports for and accommodation to the counseling function can enhance its efficacy, reduce error, improve counselor comfort, and make the gray areas a good deal lighter. In conclusion, management must come to look on the development of supervisory skills in the same way it does other skills—that is, as a basic continuing organizational responsibility and as a matter of individual career development.

The Limits of Supervisory Counseling

For our purposes, the counseling of employees by supervisors is limited by two factors: the bounds of organizational interest and the technical-interpersonal capabilities of the supervisor-counselor. Employee counseling is a desired function within the limits of legitimate organizational interest, which is to say that any problem relating to the legitimate concerns of the organization is a suitable object for counseling. This, of course, turns attention back to the question of what defines a job-related problem. Our answer to that remains the same: no simple, universal rule can be stated that will substitute for supervisory judgment. Nevertheless, some conception of the limits of organizational interest needs to be arrived at as a prerequisite to appraisal of the adequacy of counseling within the enterprise.

Why is such a conception necessary? Any supervisor, whether he knows it or not, will be limited by the level and extent of his technical counseling skills in the number and kinds of problems for which he can counsel employees. Presumably, these limits can be expanded by suitable training and/or selection procedures, but any limitation of counseling attributable to counselor deficiencies will be artificial if these limits fall short of those that would be set by the bounds of organizational interest. Following a kind of maximization principle, I am saying that it should be an organizational objective to increase the level of available counseling skill to encompass any and all problems within the boundaries of organizational interest. Optimally, in other words, the limits to counseling set by counselor skill should coincide with those set by the bounds of legitimacy. Thus the latter becomes a criterion for evaluating the aggregative level of counseling skill available to the organization as a system resource. At the very least, we must be prepared to recognize that a problem *might* be of no concern to the organization.

My references to areas of legitimacy suggest a further point. A question of some moment for the counseling function has to do with who must *initiate* the counseling relationship. Should the supervisor wait for the solicitation of the employee or may he seek the relationship? The professional counselor, of course, typically follows the former course. But since I have already defined counseling as a supervisory function, it would seem to follow that there will be many times when the supervisor will have a positive responsibility to seek the relationship *even in the face of apparent subordinate disinclination.* The employee, to be sure, is free to resist or to refuse entirely to play the game, but it is not the cooperation of the employee that defines the supervisor's responsibilities. These are defined by his job and the boundaries of organizational interest that legitimate his activities. The acceptability of supervisor initiative in counseling is obvious when a clear deficiency is evident in the subordinate's work performance. But let's consider a less obvious example.

Imagine a clerical employee whose technical performance is altogether satisfactory and who has expressed supervisory aspirations. He has recently grown a beard, which he maintains in a meticulous state of repair. His immediate supervisor, however, has reason to think that the employee's beard is prejudicial to his future in the organization because of the attitudes of certain members of the review panel responsible for selecting management trainees.

This is actually a familiar kind of case. The question is whether it is part of the supervisor's responsibility to counsel this employee about the matter of his personal appearance. It would seem that the answer should be an equivocal yes. It is equivocal because any manager is wise to have some trepidation about these personal involvements and about overextending the bounds of organizational interest. In this area, a conservative posture seems desirable. Yet, in an employee-centered framework, the supervisor has a responsibility *to the subordinate* that is not served by silence. Furthermore, assuming it to be one of the supervisor's normal functions to participate in management development, his active responsibility as an agent of the organization is plain.

Now let it be clearly understood that the chief point of this discussion is not that supervisors should try to counsel their subordinates whether they want it or not, although that is sometimes true. The point is to wed the counseling function to the larger, more inclusive supervisory function so that it reflects the same pattern of responsibilities and restrictions as the global role does—no more but no less.

Employee Counseling versus Psychotherapy

I have already said several times that employee counseling is not a kind of auxiliary psychiatry, even if it may occasionally touch incidentally on psychiatric issues and (as Dickson's list of counseling problems in work settings suggests) run up against psychiatric problems. Employee counseling, to state it bluntly again, is not psychotherapy. This point cannot be overemphasized. There are important differences, at least of emphasis, that separate therapy from counseling, as it is here envisaged. For one thing, nearly all approaches to psychotherapy treat its task in terms of basic change in the person. Moreover, its chief preoccupation is with mental illness. From common sense, as well as from what I have already said, it should be evident that neither of these perspectives is appropriate to general employee counseling.

Certainly it is true that there will be times when the supervisor-counselor will encounter significant psychiatric problems among his subordinates. In some instances, these will spill over to produce the work-related problems that bring them within the scope of supervisory responsibility. The supervisor needs, therefore, to be able to recognize such problems and to be keenly aware of his limitations in their face.

Fortunately, such difficulties are not very frequent, though they may be dramatic when they occur and therefore remembered and exaggerated. Actually, because of their comparative infrequency, the supervisor is commonly able to recognize rather quickly when he is becoming involved with psychiatric problems. He can sense it in the kinds of things the employee talks about, in the ways he talks about them, in the frequency with which he finds himself counseling with the employee, and so on. He may not be able to specify the exact nature of the disturbance, but the supervisor can usually trust his judgment as to when he is facing a problem based on an employee's disturbed personality and therefore beyond the scope of his counseling capabilities. Mistakes will be made, of course, and once more the importance of providing supervision and support for the supervisor is underscored.

The work supervisor will be wise to avoid extensive grappling with real personality disturbances. However, in practice, he is probably more likely to err in the opposite direction—that is, to avoid counseling employees from fear of encountering psychiatric problems or because of a faulty or overgeneralized conception of mental illness. Many times, too, the bugbear of mental illness will serve as a convenient rationalization for not counseling.

The regularity with which supervisors can ordinarily expect to encounter psychiatric problems sufficiently severe to cause concern will be low. However, it is worth noting that the frequency with which supervisors are called on to deal with employees having psychiatric problems is apt to increase in view of newer psychiatric-treatment orientations that strive to maintain people in their home environments and on the job. That some subordinates have psychiatric problems may complicate the supervisor's counseling job, but it certainly needn't make it impossible, any more than would the fact of cardiac disorder in a subordinate. For one thing, the fact that an individual has a psychiatric problem often has no real implications for his performance on the job, and, unless it does, it is of no concern to the supervisor. Sometimes, though, job performance will be affected in one way or another, and that fact makes desirable some managerial sophistication about psychiatric affairs. It is important for the supervisor to be able to recognize when he is dealing with a psychiatric problem, how that might affect his relations with the employee, and what alternatives exist for handling the problem.

Before turning expressly to these matters, another observation is worthy of brief mention: the supervisor-counselor is not a therapist; on that we surely can agree. His interpersonal goals are more circumscribed than that. Nonetheless, by his activities, he may contribute to elevation of the community's level of mental health. Keeping in mind the vital importance of a man's job to his sense of identity, feelings of personal worth, and whole personality organization, it can be seen that, as an outgrowth of attempts to humanize organizations, counseling may play an important part in the maintenance of mental health and the prevention of disorder. Its public-health contributions to the social scene could in the long run even outstrip those of psychiatry.

How Personality Problems Affect Counseling

There are probably four main ways in which personality problems may affect the supervisory counseling relationship: (1) they may entail risk to the supervisor and/or employee; (2) they may simply make counseling difficult; (3) they may make problems incapable of resolution; or (4) they may make counseling categorically impossible.

In the last instance, the employee's disturbance may make it impossible for him to commit himself to a counseling relationship, or it may not be possible to engage in the basically rational problem-solving that is the object of employee counseling as distinct from therapy. Or, as might be true of an employee with paranoid delusions of persecution, it may not be possible to create the level of trust necessary to counseling. In any event, the supervisor should soon become aware of the elusiveness of the relationship and develop the sense that he is "banging his head against a stone wall." Either signal is sufficient to prompt careful evaluation of the relationship, the problem, and the latter's causes (although the supervisor needs to be sure it is the employee's problems and not his own that are at the root of the difficulty).

Sometimes it may be possible to form a counseling relationship but difficult to end it because the problems never seem to move closer to resolution. In such situations it is easy to explain away supervisor inadequacies by labeling the employee mentally disturbed. However, genuine instances may arise, as in the case of an employee characterized by compulsive doubt, when, even though the problem seems to be within his potential control, no resolution occurs despite his apparent motivation. Such situations, too, call for careful evaluation of the counseling relationship.

To conclude, the fact that personality disorders may make counseling difficult is obvious. It is fundamentally a straightforward matter of skill and ability. In a way, the matter of risk is the same kind of issue; it is simply there. But it is there in all human relationships, is not very frequent anyway, and just calls for some skill in recognition and handling. The supervisor-counselor needs to be alert and discerning in evaluating problems and the people who have them. He and the enterprise should be alive to his limitations, and ideally the individual supervisor should be provided with organizational means for consultation and review of his performance.

What Should Be Done with Personality Problems?

What should a manager do about personality problems he encounters? This is obviously a difficult question, for commonly there
are few alternatives, mainly because the organization provides none.
Often the best thing to do with a personality disturbance is to ignore
it. Unless it affects the job, it is none of the supervisor's business
anyway.

In other instances, it may be desirable to establish liaison with
a treatment agent or facility responsible for the employee's psychiatric rehabilitation. It is questionable, however, whether this is a supervisory responsibility. More practically, the organization might provide consultative services, either in-house or via an outside consultant with whom supervisors may discuss problem cases and through
whom employees may be encouraged to seek competent and appropriate remedial services.

Much of what should be done is plainly determined by the
individual supervisor's technical skill as a counselor. However, it
must not be forgotten that successful inclusion of counseling functions within supervisors' roles ultimately requires genuine organizational support for those functions. Organizational support is needed
in sympathetic institutional "climates" and managerial attitudes, but
also more practically in the form of structures that will facilitate
and enhance them. It makes no sense to exhort supervisors to counsel
their subordinates or to train them to do so unless the organization
is prepared to modify itself physically and functionally to support
the activity. In fact, failure to modify may open the system to risks
of very serious unforeseen negative consequences. Not only may the
counseling function not "work" and therefore leave unsolved whatever problems it was hoped would be solved by it; it may also reduce
supervisor morale by elevating their level of frustration and the like
because of their inability to perform a function for which they have
been trained and told was important and expected of them.

Some Further Thoughts on Supervisory Roles

Discussion of the enlargement of supervisory roles to include
counseling functions must eventually lead to questions about
whether it is possible or practical to mix supervisory functions the

way I have envisaged. At this time, the point quite honestly is moot; it has been insufficiently explored to give a fair answer. However, it seems likely that the two functions will mix, if only loosely. Implementation of counseling, though, will doubtless require some modification of traditional supervisory practice. I've tried to make that fact unmistakable. But what will sometimes be needed to make it possible may amount to more than shifts in attitude and style. Structural and procedural redesign may be called for. More specifically, it may prove desirable for some employee counseling to be done by persons not responsible for the employee's daily supervision. This person could still be a supervisor. It would simply be a matter of crossing supervisory lines. There is, after all, nothing sacred about traditional organizational designs. And such arrangements might sometimes help alleviate the dilemma produced by supervisor-counselors having mixed loyalties to the employee and to the organization.

What consideration of such a procedure points up is the desirability of thinking of supervision in terms of functions or roles—system resources—rather than solely in terms of the people who hold these offices. There is really nothing odd about certain supervisory functions being performed by different supervisors with reference to the same employee. It happens all the time in project or matrix types of organizations, for instance. In any event, attempts to implement employee-centered management precepts ought to occasion searching appraisals of the assumptions that underlie organizational operations and designs.

Conclusion

In this chapter I have mentioned a number of ideas, concepts, and problems associated with the counseling of employees by supervisors. From a distance, these problems and the impediments to counseling they imply may look immense. The initial response to them tends to be one of futility. I have been encouraged, however, by the fact that the more closely one looks at them the more manageable the problems appear and the more optimistic one tends to feel about their satisfactory solution. It is not at all unreasonable to expect substantial improvement in the scope and quality of employee counseling as a function of improved orientation, training, and organizational adaptation.

However, nothing is more important to the development of supervisors as counselors than the comprehensive description of the functions I call counseling. Indeed, it is basic. The concept of counseling is a vague one in general, and adding the adjective "employee" hasn't improved matters. We shall need to develop a consensus about the purposes, processes, and procedures of employee counseling so that we can teach the appropriate skills, evaluate their performance, and settle counseling comfortably in working and developing organizational contexts. Here we have touched on this issue only tentatively, indirectly, or by implication, but it is the paramount concern of the next chapter and those that follow it.

References

Bijou, S. W. Implications of behavioral science for counseling and guidance. In J. D. Krumboltz (Ed.), *Revolution in counseling*. Boston: Houghton Mifflin, 1966.

Dickson, W. J., & Roethlisberger, F. J. *Counseling in an organization*. Cambridge, Mass.: Harvard University Press, 1966.

Dowling, W. F., Jr., & Sayles, L. R. *How managers motivate: The imperatives of supervision*. New York: McGraw-Hill, 1971.

Homans, G. *The human group*. New York: Harcourt Brace Jovanovich, 1950.

Hunt, R. G., & Lichtman, C. "Counseling" of employees by work supervisors: Concepts, attitudes, and practices in a white-collar organization. *Journal of Counseling Psychology*, 1969, **16,** 81–86.

Krumboltz, J. D. Behavioral counseling: Rationale and research. In S. H. Osipow & W. B. Walsh (Eds.), *Behavior change in counseling: Readings and cases*. New York: Appleton-Century-Crofts, 1970. Pp. 14–21.

Osipow, S. H., & Walsh, W. B. *Strategies in counseling for behavior change*. New York: Appleton-Century-Crofts, 1970.

Perrow, C. *Complex organizations: A critical essay*. Glenview, Ill.: Scott, Foresman, 1972.

Roethlisberger, F. J., & Dickson, W. J. *Management and the worker*. Cambridge, Mass.: Harvard University Press, 1939.

Recommended Readings

Dunnette, M. D., & Kirchner, W. K. *Psychology applied to industry*. New York: Appleton-Century-Crofts, 1965. (A valuable little book, see Chapter 4 for a discussion of counseling in industry.)

Kunze, K. R. Employment outlook for counselors in business and industry. *Personnel and Guidance Journal*, in press. (This review of counseling activity in work environments was scheduled to appear in the September 1973 issue of the *Journal*. It is a useful documentation of the comparative rarity of such activities by the head of industrial relations of the California-Lockheed Co., who went to some lengths to find out what was happening.)

Lofquist, L. H., & Dawes, R. V. *Application of the theory of work adjustment to rehabilitation and counseling*. Minnesota Studies in Vocational Rehabilitation: XX. University of Minnesota Industrial Relations Center, June 1972. (A general review of the Minnesota Work Adjustment Project that includes bibliographies, descriptions of questionnaires, tests, and other instruments as well as discussion of relations between counseling and worker job satisfaction.)

Mobilization for Youth. *Publications list*. The Experimental Manpower Laboratory, 271 E. 4th Street, New York, N.Y. 10009. (Cites, in annotated form, a wide variety of reports and documents having to do with the use of counseling methods especially in developing more effective work attitudes and behavior among the disadvantaged.)

Oetting, E. R., & Cole, C. W. Job coaching: The effect on work adjustment of the disadvantaged. Unpublished manuscript. Colorado State University Experimental Manpower Laboratory, Fort Collins, Colorado. (An experimental examination of a counseling-type approach to the improvement of job performance. It shows the importance of developing programs that concentrate on affecting specific behaviors or attitudinal manifestations.)

Wrenn, C. G. Human values and work in American life. In H. Borrow (Ed.), *Man in a world at work*. Boston: Houghton Mifflin, 1964. (A cogent statement of the importance of work in personality organization. The book as a whole is worthwhile.)

Counseling
Goals and
Methods

One of the more unorthodox of the early psychoanalysts, Otto Rank, once remarked without humor that his technique of therapy consisted of having no technique. By this he meant that he sought to avoid treating people according to standardized routines and rigidly applied formulas. He preferred, instead, to suit his methods more pragmatically to the particular circumstances of individual cases. His stress was always on the therapist's need to recognize and cope with the unique amalgamations of persons and events that emerge in even the most prosaic and seemingly familiar circumstances. Rank saw the therapist's task essentially as one of helping with the solution of problems by fostering establishment of a cohesive working relation with the patient. Doing that, he felt, depended on his recognizing the patient's individuality and remaining free to adapt his methods of therapy to the emerging needs of the particular relationship.

Similar impatience with standardized techniques has been popular among modern-day counselors. Impatience was often expressed by practitioners of the "client-centered" school of counseling (see Rogers, 1951). Also, Krumboltz (who belongs to quite a different school) remarked in connection with his definition of counseling, mentioned in the previous chapter, that it deliberately left unspecified the methods to be used. As Robert Callis (1970) sensibly argues, the counselor's techniques have to be no less varied than the problems he encounters.

Enterprise management and work supervision also require techniques varied to suit different problems. Effective management involves the integration of distinctive organizational goals, special technical requirements, and personal idiosyncracies into productive and personally rewarding operational blends. There can be no best method of management, no managerial Holy Grail. The exact ways good managers go about their jobs are, and surely must remain, highly varied in operational detail. Flexibility, adaptability, and other pertinent characteristics may be identified as hallmarks of superior managerial styles and practices. However, these characteristics will always be expressed as syntheses of general management principles and objectives with special skills and personal attributes that lend individualized colorations to managerial modes.

When applied to problems of management and supervision, the counseling perspective must take account of these realities. If there is no single true method of management, neither is there any one universal counseling technique. It should come as no surprise to learn that good managers generally make good counselors and *vice versa*. Most especially, gimmicks and gambits have no place in sound counseling repertories.

Yet methods must exist by which counseling concepts can be implemented. After all, counseling involves teachable interpersonal skills. The point to be understood is that the nature of these skills and methods is to be found mainly in the form of guidelines, points of reference, broad procedural orientations, and what the psychologists term "mental sets," rather than in highly specific standard routines and rules for their application.

Counseling Strategies

The fundamental goals of counseling can be stated simply enough:

1. To reduce levels of anxiety prevalent in work environments and to accomplish increased comfort and morale on the parts of organization members.
2. To increase the self-respect and self-confidence of organization members.
3. To lower the degrees of defensiveness among organization

members, thereby helping to open channels of communication.

4. To enhance the system's overall problem-solving ability and hence its effectiveness and productivity.

Even stated so simply, it must be evident that many means of reaching those goals must exist.

The matter of counseling technique is a difficult one by definition, for counseling has to do principally with nonroutine problem-solving—with the so-called unprogrammed functions of management. Effective performance of these functions entails a basic freedom from presumption and standardization and a disposition toward invention and experimentation. Probably the most effective way to think of counseling methods, therefore, is in terms of strategies, the tactical implementation of which will depend largely on ingenuity and the personal styles of individual supervisors. What works with striking effect for one counselor in a given circumstance may be unnatural or unsuited for another. In short, each supervisor must develop his own techniques, forging and sharpening them with practice.

When founded on a sure grasp of the strategies of counseling and articulated with a supporting philosophy of management, each supervisor's individualized panoply of counseling methods constitutes an alternative mode of expression equally as right and acceptable as any other based on the same premises. If the supervisor can be provided with an opportunity to practice his newly emerging skills under supervision and as part of a systematic supportive program, so much the better. But in any event, he must be wary of a preoccupation with technique and can expect no simple procedural rules of thumb or human-relations routines that he can perform "by the numbers." The essential question, then, as a preliminary to developing sound counseling practices, is: What are the fundamental strategies of counseling?

Collaboration and Management in the Counseling Relationship

Counseling is first and foremost a collaborative problem-solving undertaking. It is strategically directed to the clear and precise identification of problems, the generation of suitable alternative solutions to those problems, the reasoned choice from among the alternatives generated, and the subsequent evaluation of the organizational adequacy of the chosen alternative. I view counseling as a fundamentally rational operation—one that is, furthermore, a disciplined one. Disciplined not in the sense of autocratic, hierarchical control but in the sense of its being an orderly, managed process.

Counseling is not an occasion for a random bull session nor for the cathartic ventilation of personal sentiments, although simple conversation and emotional expression do have a prospective place in the counseling scheme. They may, for example, serve as information-gathering devices, or they may simply be necessary to the development and maintenance of the interpersonal counseling relationship. But like any other particular counseling event or method, they are means to the problem-solving goal, not ends in themselves. Counseling itself is a purposive supervisory activity, and it is the responsibility of the supervisor to manage it with point and wisdom, a matter to which we shall return subsequently.

For the moment, we can say that constructive management of the counseling relationship requires the commitment and involvement of both the counselor and the counseled as active participants. Joint problem-solving and an atmosphere of mutuality are fundamental to its success. The subordinate, no less than the superior, must function as an authentic member of a problem-solving, decision-making unit and not as a mere passive object of counseling. Provision of the conditions, organizational as well as attitudinal, necessary to assure this collaboration is a primary managerial responsibility. Administrative despotism or paternalism, however well-intentioned, is an institutional frame of reference ill-suited to counseling and productive problem-solving.

As with management systems generally, I believe counseling to be most effective when conceived and conducted democratically, which is to say participatively. Unquestionably, it is sufficient to justify participative strategies on moral-social grounds, but they are defensible on organizational grounds, too. Broadly based, decentralized control and decision systems tend to yield more timely decisions and decrease the load on communicative channels at the same time that they increase the availability of relevant information. Furthermore, as we know, participation fosters a feeling of "we-ness" and contributes to the development by employees of Drucker's "managerial attitude." Thus, to repeat one more time, participative methodologies are practical as well as desirable management strategies.

Counseling and Change

Counseling is a problem-solving process, but a forward-looking, change-oriented one. It seeks solutions to immediate problems with an orientation toward preventing their recurrence. Finding more effective means of solving future problems and generally helping the system to grow and to function more effectively are among the principal objectives of counseling. Hence counseling seeks to involve the members of an enterprise in a collaborative quest for problems and their immediate solution and, in the process, creates a vehicle for learning and development, both individual and organizational.

The counseling relationship, therefore, must work with an eye to the future. One can learn from the past, to be sure, and viewing present problems against a backdrop of their history is vital to their comprehensive understanding. But in operational systems, history is important mainly for the lessons it supplies for the future. As such, the past is merely that—past. Dwelling on it can serve no useful organizational purpose. It follows, therefore, that the organizationally pertinent question to be asked about any problem is: What can be done about it?

Counseling and Blame

A corollary of this prospective principle is the idea that counseling cannot flourish in a blame-oriented managerial climate. Ideally, problems are to be identified and analyzed not so as to affix blame for them but as essential points of departure in seeking their solution.

Our natural proclivities toward passing judgments on other people's actions or feelings—that is, to evaluate them solely or primarily from our own frame of reference—stands as one of the most persistent yet unnecessary impediments to easy, free interpersonal communication. It is also one of the principal reasons why people routinely assume defensive postures even before anything has happened: they quite sensibly assume that the worst will happen because it has so often in the past.

Detailed analysis of problems may often lead to questions about their causes—questions that connect with matters of institutional or personal responsibility. The point of such questions is to illuminate directions, strategies, and tactics for individual and system improvement, not to select targets for punishment or chastisement. In short, the counseling relationship, to be maximally effective, needs to avoid a punitive coloration and must endeavor instead to foster task-oriented feelings of confidence, common respect, and trust. The supervisor-counselor will find that reinforcing the positive is a more productive tactic than punishment or its threat.

Counseling and Human Relationships

Basic to modern management and counseling methods are human relationships. They constitute both the settings for management and counseling and the instruments by which the goals of enterprise are achieved. The one clearly indispensable long-run ingredient of viable and effective organizations is the facilitative effect, at all levels, of high-quality supervisory relationships. Indeed, the paramount task of management can be described as the development and nourishment of satisfying, productive working relations throughout the enterprise. In more technical terms, these relationships typically mark and mediate the functional interfaces among system components; skillful management of those interfaces is crucial to effective system performance.

How this is done will vary, of course, with time, place, and personnel. At base, however, it comes down to a matter of simple human decency and its expression. Certainly, a supportive framework of underlying attitudes is fundamental. These include a genuine willingness and preparedness to help and, yes, to take help, together with respect for the essential dignity, integrity, individuality, and capabilities of the subordinate. Given these dispositions as bedrock, reciprocal trust can be built and easy and productive working relations facilitated.

Counseling Methods

Essential as they may be, in practice it takes more than good thoughts, feelings of warm humanity, and a prickly conscience to build effective relations. It takes skill and effort, and that is what counseling, as a *method* of management, is all about. In that sense, counseling employees is the skillful communication of humane, democratic, and relationship-building sentiments while performing a productive task. Its essentials are a series of keystones of counseling. As the term implies, each of these keystones is conceived as architecturally or structurally essential to the counseling process and to the supervisory relationship. Each one is a basic component of counseling method, and collectively they define the procedural essence of counseling and the basic principles of participation in management.

Counseling Keystones

LISTENING

The counseling concept implies a genuine interest in the other person. This interest includes a sincere desire to help, to see the other fellow's point of view, to understand. Furthermore, as a problem-solving process, counseling is a means for obtaining, evaluating, and making use of information. Careful attention to inputs other than one's own is therefore basic to its success. For these reasons, cultivation of the art of listening (which includes a willingness to be influenced by what is heard) is crucial to the attainment of the goals of counseling and to development of satisfactory supervisory relations.

Some supervisors, however, think of their jobs almost exclusively in terms of telling people what to do. For these supervisors, encounters with employees consist largely of giving orders, exhortations, and reprimands or of making announcements. They tend to feel that they must serve as an inexhaustible font of wisdom, prepared at all times to solve problems by pronouncement. Even when the employee is talking, such supervisors are preoccupied with what they plan to say instead of with listening carefully.

Regular failures to develop information vital to the accurate diagnosis of problems and to the planning of their solutions result from this form of supervisory malpractice. Furthermore, the pontifical posture does little to communicate any real interest in the employee or his problems and so does little to enhance the supervisory relationship. Nor does it stimulate identification with the organization or augment motivation to perform within it.

Effective counseling, in contrast, involves taking time to encourage the employee to discuss matters of interest to him and listening when he does. He is worth listening to: rational decision-making depends on the kind of feedback obtainable only by listening. In conversation with a subordinate, such simple remarks by a supervisor as "that's really interesting, George; could you tell me more about what you mean?" tend to elicit a lot more useful information than more cursory counterparts, such as "how about that" or "yeah, I know." In addition, the former statement implies respect for the subordinate's judgment and concern with building a real working relationship.

People often leave more implied than they actually say. Admittedly, sometimes that's for the best. But an effective supervisor will seek nonthreatening ways for judicious use in helping to establish conditions under which employees can give voice to matters of mutual concern that otherwise would remain unspoken. The employee complaining about being docked for tardiness may never get a chance to state the fullness of the reasons for his irritation or the reasons for his lateness unless someone takes the time and effort to do more than lecture him about company policy and the fact that "I've got a department to run." Furthermore, the likelihood of a lasting solution to the problem of tardiness is lessened.

It must be realized that counseling demands more than mere passive listening. It demands active efforts to understand the other person. Henry Clay Smith, in his *Sensitivity to People* (1966), emphasizes the same point, aptly classifying listening as a special case of the more general process of *observing*. Without understanding, the whole listening/observation process reduces to a colossal waste of time. And one of the most dangerous things a counselor can do is to assume he understands and then to base his actions on that assumption without confirming its validity. To ask the other person "do you mean that . . . ?" or "are you saying that . . . ?" or something like it is a simple matter. "I'm not sure I understand; perhaps you could tell me more about or explain it further" may insure the counselor against serious error. At the same time, it communicates his interest and willingness at least to try to understand his associates and to act on that understanding, rather than exclusively on his own predilections.

There is one problem point to remember: many of the verbal probes or other methods mentioned here and elsewhere in this chapter (for example, "there's a problem here, Jean, that I need your help with") can degenerate into gimmicks, gambits, and manipulative ploys designed not to convey genuine interest or concern but to con the subordinate into trust in the boundless good will of the boss or into thinking what a great guy he is. Such perversions, along with the reflexive, nondiscriminating use of buzz-words and phrases ("let me share with you . . ." or "hey, that's really interesting . . .")

not backed by substance authenticated in action, are simply self-defeating in the not-very-long run.

TWO-WAY COMMUNICATION

The supervisory relation is an important, indeed critical, link in an organization's communication network. The supervisor's role in the downward flow of information has, of course, traditionally been recognized. Less emphasis, however, has been given the more difficult task of fostering effective upward communication. Our concept of the supervisory relation as a process of joint problem-solving is intended to highlight the importance of communication processes, to underscore the equal significance of upward and downward communication, and to direct attention to the contribution of effective supervisory relations in making communication processes successful.

Thus, developing and maintaining effective communication within the organization are vital supervisory/managerial functions. Their implementation depends on mutual give-and-take between two or more parties, supervisor and subordinates. Because good communication is a two-way process, it requires that the supervisor become a good listener, but it also requires that he accept responsibility for being understood when he speaks.

This means that he must work at communication, thinking about what he wants to say and how he will say it to assure that the message gets across as he intends it. Unfortunately, sometimes what we intend to communicate and the actual message a listener receives are two quite different things.

To be sure, this often happens because somebody failed to listen, but just as often it results from the speaker being concerned with *what* he wants to say but neglectful of *how* he says it (or when he says it). Too often, speakers assume that one word is like another. Consequently, messages get sent that do not truly reflect the sender's intention—messages that may defeat the speaker's objectives or even undermine the whole relationship, especially if emotions are aroused. When determining the message that is actually communicated, the form of the message, especially its wording, must be treated as no less important than its intended content. The form of the message goes a long way toward determining the "tone" of the communication and hence toward governing the "positive" or "negative" quality of the exchange.

In other words, the interests of good communication oblige the supervisor to become a careful speaker as well as an attentive listener, for it is not only what is said but how it is said that counts. Archie Bunkers are funny on television, but they are a lot less so when they are your boss. This is perhaps most vividly evident when it is necessary, as it frequently is, to deal with sensitive or unpleasant issues within the supervisory relationship. However, as a general principle, it is germane to even the most pedestrian of exchanges.

Starting a discussion of a missed production schedule with the assertion that "things will shape up around here or some people will ship out!" is obviously an inauspicious beginning. It might strike terror into the hearts of subordinates and boldly etch power relations, but otherwise all it does is elicit defensiveness, tendencies to allocate (or misallocate) blame, and desires to leave the situation. As an approach to problem-solving, it definitely is not recommended.

Unfortunately, the type of message that will promote effective problem-solving in a particular case is not always subject to determination by standard operating procedures. Once more, success finally depends on the essential wisdom and humanity of the supervisor, the time he has taken to understand the people working with him, and his preparation for individualizing supervision. For example, a conscientious white supervisor in the present world will almost certainly approach disciplinary problems involving black subordinates differently from the way he would approach the same problems among whites. The difference in approach is not because of skin color but because of the differences in the life situations of black and white workers; viewed in full perspective, their problems are not really the same, and so they need different, individualized handling.

COMMUNICATOR OPENNESS

There are exceptions to the rule, but as a generality it can be assumed that things will go better when the parties to a relationship know reasonably well where they stand with one another. This is another way of saying that good communication and the growth of sound supervisory relations presuppose an essential personal honesty. The parties to the relationship must be prepared to deal openly with matters vital to it, even when these are unpleasant. Critical performance evaluations, to cite but one example, cannot be shirked, because to do so undermines the candor and trust on which the relationship is premised.

The kind of frank and forthright conduct of affairs that a critical performance evaluation implies can, however, easily degenerate into insults and injury. It is bad enough when leveling is used as an excuse or a rationalization for aggression, but when pain inflicted on another is inadvertent, it is a tragedy. Managerial competence rests on sensitivity, tact, and empathy as much as (or more than) it does on technical proficiency. Understanding and attention to styles and forms as well as to content are prerequisite to constructively open interpersonal relations and effective organizational communication. That only sticks and stones can hurt is a myth; words can be weapons as well as building blocks.

A kind of corollary to the openness keystone is the idea of communicator timeliness. The rule of thumb is: getting to it sooner is better than later. And the worse it is, the better it is the sooner it is (understanding, of course, that impulsive actions are almost always poor ones, so that a sense of proportion is assumed). Allowing problems to fester or to become chronic by putting off dealing with them risks creating volatile working environments in which a trivial spark can set off cataclysmic interpersonal explosions and in which supervisors then find themselves obliged to justify their overreaction by elevating matters of simple operational routine to the status of high moral principle. This does nothing but disfigure and foul up the whole problem-solving process. It is under such conditions that one gets supervisory outbursts such as "Dammit, Charley, you just won't cooperate at all with what we're trying to do around here! We've got policies around here, but you always want to go off on your own and do whatever you wish!" Such an outburst often occurs when Charley doesn't know what he has been doing wrong or how the magnitude of his boss's reaction relates to the importance of his own acts.

Probably the worst violation of the timeliness corollary occurs when, after years of employment, the first inkling a person gets of long-term dissatisfaction with his work comes when he's told he's fired.

ACCENTUATING THE POSITIVE

A substantial portion of supervisor-employee interchange centers around problems. And much of that centers around some real or suspected subordinate performance deficiency. Obviously, there is no way to evade this ineluctable organizational reality, and it is undesirable to try. If the supervisor construes his responsibility to his organization in a developmental sense, however, it follows that

that responsibility extends to include his subordinates and their "deficiencies," defined as problems to be solved. As with other problems, little in the way of development is likely if performance critiques are exclusively a matter of pointing out how the employee blew it again. That just states what everybody already knew, in addition to getting things off on a negative footing calculated to make the employee defensive at best.

A constructive performance critique pivots on finding the employee's strong points that can be built on to increase his capabilities and thus enhance the resources available to the system. Forward-looking problem-solving will pay at least as much attention to what went right as it will to what went wrong. It is as important organizationally to strengthen what's going well as it is to fix what's not. We shall come back to these ideas again in a later chapter but I want to point out now that building solid working relations and building (or at least not tearing down) employee confidence and self-respect go together. There may well be times when a supervisor will have to go out of his way to find something positive to reinforce (at minimum, it can frequently be said at the start "I know this was really a tough job . . ."). Sometimes the detour may be too long to justify the trip. But, barring extremities, the diversion can often be the best part of the journey.

There is also a corollary to this idea of accentuating the positive. A supervisor may find a well-placed simple word of encouragement, a pat on the back, or an expression of recognition more powerful tools for motivating employee performance on a day-by-day basis than just about anything else he can dispense, including money.

DEALING WITH EMOTIONS

Successful supervision requires tact and sensitivity, as I have said. But it can be defeated by an excess of timidity. Any relationship worth its salt, whatever its nature, will generate emotions on the parts of its members. Not all of these will be joyful or even calm and tranquil. People become angry and depressed as well as placid, pleased, or euphoric. And they're likely to be more emotional in relations that are important to them.

It is inappropriate, certainly, to stimulate emotion for its own sake. After all, we are seeking the nurturance of rational problem-solving. But neither should we seek totally to avoid or suppress all expressions of feeling. Good communication and the preservation of sound supervisory relations depend on recognizing emotions when they are there and being willing, if not eager, to deal with them. Nor should the idea that counseling is aimed at reducing anxiety and tension be taken as justification for evading confrontation with anxiety-producing topics or circumstances (or the evidences of tension in the expressions of others). As a rule of thumb, all parties to a relationship should leave any encounter feeling better (or at least no worse) than they did at the outset. Getting to that objective, however, may require crossing some occasionally rugged emotional terrain.

That I stress the significance of dealing actively with *irrational* aspects of people's natures at the same time that I have identified supervisory counseling as cardinally *rational* is no paradox. Among the most common reasons for communication failures and relationship breakdowns are problems of recognizing and handling feelings. Admittedly, this is difficult. People shy away from emotions (at least from the negative ones). Most people tend to become anxious when confronted by feelings and are prone to react defensively. Typical reactions consist of leaving the company of the emotional person, endeavoring to shut off the display of feeling, avoiding subjects calculated to arouse emotions in the first place, and a host of familiar strategems. Yet it must be possible in sound, productive relationships to express feelings that are relevant to it. It does no good to stifle them or to react to emotion by rushing to the defense of one's own positions or actions, as supervisors all too characteristically do. None of these attitudes or practices is suitable in an optimal supervisory relation. Feelings are natural parts of life; they need to be ventilated, tolerated, explored, and modulated from time to time, but not avoided.

Sustaining Focus in Counseling

Earlier I described employee counseling as a problem-focused operation. I suggested, for one thing, that it was ordinarily inappropriate for work supervisors to become deeply involved with the personalities of their subordinates. For another, I have proposed counseling as a participative method for solving problems and making decisions. Operationally, therefore, the supervisor-counselor has a critical responsibility for sustaining the focus of the relationship on the problems with which it is concerned. Furthermore, in any task-oriented setting, time (especially managerial time) must be employed with wise and purposeful economy.

Yet it is easy and more or less natural to allow conversational relations to roam through interesting and attractive by-ways. Sometimes, in fact, such may even be the purpose of a problem-solving relation—as, for instance, when the shape or dimensions of a problem are vague and poorly understood. Sometimes, too, such procedural looseness is essential as a relationship-building activity. The point, however, is that what is done in the relationship is generally done for a purpose appropriate to its larger function and that there commonly exist criteria of relevance with which to appraise the cogency of contents. It is the responsibility of the supervisor to make those appraisals with tact, sensitivity, and concern for the long-term viability of the relationship.

There is no useful end served by sacrificing the supervisory relationship on an altar of rigid requirements of relevance. Yet it is important that the relationship not be allowed to drift until it loses its thread, lacks point, or becomes indecisive. This is a very difficult thing to do well, but to maximize the impact of counseling and to conduct it economically the supervisor must endeavor to understand what is happening in the relationship and to guide it so as to sustain the crispness of its focus.

To illustrate the point: imagine a technically capable supervisor meeting with his own supervisor about the fact that his work group shows clear signs of poor morale (turnover, absenteeism, requests for transfer, and so on):

> *Manager:* Ok, let's see if we can at least come up with a preliminary idea about just what the problem is. I expect we have to begin really with whether you want to continue in the job. Clearly your technical qualifications are outstanding, but it isn't going to work out if the people working with you are tense and upset all the time.
>
> *Supervisor:* Are you telling me you might replace me?
>
> *Manager:* Not now; but you know as well as I that it could come to that. Right now what I'm asking is how *you* feel about staying on as supervisor.
>
> *Supervisor:* Well, the truth is I've thought about it. I liked my job before and didn't have all the hassles. But I think I can be a good supervisor. I just don't know I guess.

Manager: There isn't much we can do until we get some resolution of that. And we'll have to talk about it. But in the meantime maybe we could talk about just what you see as the problems in your group and what we need to do about them.

Many, if not most, problems present themselves in bunches or with their outlines blurred. No relationship can deal with all problems at once or deal effectively with any problem until it has some clarity of conception. A critical initial step in the counseling process, therefore, has to do with the identification, clarification, separation, and selection of the problems to which attention and energy will be directed. The parties to the relationship can and should devote sufficient time to the discussion of these issues, selecting change targets and assigning priorities to them. I said before that counseling was a disciplined process; planning is a major part of that discipline.

The productive identification and selection of problems or change targets depend on their translation into *concrete* terms. In the first place, they are easier to understand by more people in that form. Furthermore, specific targets are more likely to be achieved than are diffuse ones. Generally speaking, this dictum means that change targets should be stated as much as possible in specific behavioral terms. The basic question in the relationship then becomes: What behavior is to be changed and what behavior is to replace it? The more exact the answers to these questions are, the more likely is success.

EVALUATING SOLUTIONS

There is another reason for concretizing and, as argued in Chapter 4, relating change targets to the levels of their application. Only then can their achievement be clearly appraised (and their separate consequences effectively integrated). Every change program, however simple or grand, should include means for its monitoring and evaluation. This, too, is difficult. Easy means are not always available, and it is often hard to get agreement about suitable modes of assessment. Yet my philosophy of management requires some consensus about criteria for evaluation. Indeed, obtaining such consensus was a prominent part of the development strategy outlined in Chapter 4. No one really accepts the results of assessment when he disagrees with the methods used. Thus another early step in the counseling process must center around the discovery of mutually acceptable criteria for evaluating performance and change and for monitoring the process. This step will be easier to take and will almost certainly have more fruitful issue when it has been preceded by a careful and specific statement of problems and/or individual change targets.

At this juncture, I can probably summarize our discussion of the crucial process of sustaining focus in counseling by stating a checklist of questions each supervisor-counselor might routinely ask himself (or be asked by his supervisor) as he approaches or reviews a particular counseling relation or episode:

1. What exactly is the problem?
2. How is it manifest in the work setting? What various concrete forms does it take?
3. What is the significance of the problem? What are its personal and organizational implications? What different organizational operations or concerns does it affect and how? Does it deserve or require attention and how urgently in comparison with other matters? What is the status of the working relations (including my own) among the people involved? Are there problems? Does anything need to be done about them? What?
4. What can or might be done about it? What alternatives exist? What resources do each of them require?
5. So far as it can be foretold, what outcomes can be expected from each prospective solution? What side-effects might they have?
6. From among the alternatives discriminated, which seems to be the best? Why? Which of them would at least be satisfactory?
7. How can the effects of the proposed solution be monitored and evaluated? What period of time will be allocated to trial? What can be done in the event of failure?

Faithful attention to providing answers to these questions can only enhance the counseling/problem-solving/decision-making process. Among other things, managers may learn that the most obvious solutions to problems are not always, or even often, the best.

Control of the Relationship and the Role of the Supervisor

I am describing, in this book, an image of managerial operations cast in participatory democratic terms. The employee, I have argued, has a *right* to involvement with and influence over the conditions and policies of his employment. Moreover, it is generally salutary to the operations of the system to motivate rather than to compel performance, to elicit broad participation in goal-setting, problem-solving, and decision-making, and to integrate work standards with work-group interests.

The idea that work organizations might be humane and democratic does not, however, preclude asymmetries of responsibility and influence within them. To argue so is disingenuous and to assume so is naive. What the democratic precept demands is simply that influence be legitimate and essentially commensurate with the competent exercise of responsibility.

The preceding section implies, and I have noted elsewhere, that all organizations must incorporate control systems of one kind or another to regulate subsystem interactions and the distribution and use of power (as well as other resources). Administration of these control functions and coordination of the separate activities of the system in the service of organizational objectives are legitimate managerial functions. In fact, they compose the managerial *raison d'être.*

With regard to the managerial/supervisory role and the place of counseling within it, this implies an active as opposed to a passive mode of performance. The manager, too, is an active participant in organizational processes—one with special and distinctive responsibilities. The fundamental leadership functions of management must not be forgotten in the process of avoiding their construction in autocratic terms. Supervision is a collaborative venture and counseling is a concatenation of interpersonal ideas and skills for accomplishing it within a democratic framework. But managers and supervisors have special responsibilities. The burden is on them to sustain the problem-solving focus of the supervisory relationship. It is also their responsibility to guarantee conceptualization of their particular functions in terms of larger system perspectives while meshing their immediate goals with more general organizational objectives. In short, it is a responsibility of management to know where it is going and to be capable of appropriately controlling organizational operations so as to get there.

Squaring the matter of control with democratic ideas may seem problematic, but only to those accustomed to thinking of control exclusively in terms of the raw exercise of power. What I have in mind is something altogether different. It is a concept of control cast in terms of information feedback, guidance, influence, and leadership made possible by effective supervisory performance. Aptitude and skill, technical and interpersonal, are among the concept's primary prerequisites, but an orientation toward planning is a useful way to assure its realization.

PLANNING FOR COUNSELING

There is nothing inherently inconsistent between planning and democracy, collaboration, or spontaneity. There really seems to be no good reason for a counselor or supervisor to refrain from preparation for a meeting with a subordinate. He might better, to the extent he can, reflect on the circumstances of the meeting, review its history, and try to anticipate its needs and likely events. Many counseling sessions fail because the counselor is taken by surprise by something and becomes disorganized and unable to control the direction of the relationship. Certainly it is true that one cannot expect always to be able to anticipate everything that may ensue. But it is also true that one can anticipate some of it and can at least forecast areas of uncertainty, thereby decreasing the incidence of major surprises and reducing the chances of inept performance.

Avoiding planning out of a disinclination to appear autocratic is thus no better than avoiding it out of principle, sloth, or incompetence. Effects are notoriously indifferent to their causes. Dedication to letting things take their course yields management from crisis to crisis and an absolute preoccupation with putting out fires—hardly a climate conducive to rationality. That one can become a slave to one's plans and a true-believing tyrant in the service of their execution is a useful caveat to this discussion, but it serves as a caution, not as an excuse.

Apart from preparation by the supervisor (and by the subordinate, too, for that matter) for counseling sessions, planning should be a regular topic within the supervisory relation. A large part of the joint supervisor-subordinate venture will necessarily consist of collaborative planning for its future. This, of course, has been implicit in almost everything that I have said here about counseling as a future-oriented process.

Counseling and Interviewing

Some special counseling methods will be presented later, and more attention will be given to the reinforcement principle and behavioral counseling, but from our discussion here it should be evident that, however embellished or otherwise modified, the primary vehicle for counseling and hence for supervision is the interview. A good supervisor will need to be a good interviewer.

An interview has been defined as "a conversation with a purpose." In its very brevity, that conception fits my purposes admirably, for it underscores the vital importance of sustaining purposeful postures in supervisory actions. The conversation may not always be easy to follow, running in nonverbal as well as in more familiar verbal channels, and, of course, its purposes will vary. But generally speaking, all interviews will have one or both of two purposes: giving and receiving information or attempting to influence attitudes and behavior. From variations in the emphases among their particular purposes, it is possible to distinguish several functional varieties of interview:

1. Fact-finding: obtaining information about events, people, or other circumstances. An exit interview with a terminating employee might exemplify an interview emphasizing fact-finding.
2. Information dissemination: giving information about organizational policies or the like. A group meeting to describe new procedural routines or system reorganization would illustrate this variety of interview. The fact-finding interview is concerned mainly with *upward* communication; information dissemination is directed more to *downward* communications.
3. Motivational: attempting to induce or encourage modifications in either or both the effort or direction of employee performance. Here the interviewer is frankly striving to influence attitudes or behavior. In the jargon of the times, the supervisor is adopting the role of a change agent.
4. Helping: collaborating with a subordinate in seeking solutions to problems identified or at least recognized by him as problems needful of solution. The problems for which solutions are being sought may be technical, organizational, or personal.
5. Appraisal: evaluating employees or their situations. Here the supervisor is communicating judgments about matters of interest to him (and presumably to the subordinate). Appraisal interviews are oriented to surfacing problems and should be expected to lead quickly to helping or motivational varieties.

To some extent, different methods or approaches may be called for (or highlighted anyway) in these different interview contexts.

The same overall attitude will be appropriate to all of them, however, for it must be obvious that the five varieties of interview just described point almost entirely to variations in momentary emphasis rather than to discrete types of nonoverlapping interviews. In fact, a given supervisory interview could, and many will, be conducted for a plurality of reasons. Some will include all of the functions cited.

In supervisory settings, interviewing is a way of both coming to understand people and intelligently applying that understanding to the processes of motivating and helping them. Behind the simple statement that an interview is a conversation with a purpose hides a multitude of complexities that require some artistry to master. In this chapter, I have outlined the more basic of those complexities and indicated the ingredients of the artistry their mastery requires. Let's turn now to the question of how managers can be prepared and trained as artful interviewers and successful employee counselors.

References

Callis, R. Toward an integrated theory of counseling. In S. H. Osipow & W. B. Walsh (Eds.), *Behavior change in counseling*. New York: Appleton-Century-Crofts, 1970. Pp. 4–14.

Rogers, C. R. *Client-centered therapy*. Boston: Houghton Mifflin, 1951.

Smith, H. C. *Sensitivity to people*. New York: McGraw-Hill, 1966.

Recommended Readings

Benjamin, A. *The helping interview*. Boston: Houghton Mifflin, 1969. (An artistically written paperback containing sound information on how to relate to others in an interview.)

Berne, E. *Games people play*. New York: Grolier, 1963. (The various gambits and ploys people use to manipulate one another.)

Gorden, R. *Interviewing*. Homewood, Ill.: Dorsey Press, 1969. (A thorough and thoughtful treatment of the varied problems and methods of the art.)

Shertzer, B., & Stone, S. C. *Fundamentals of counseling*. Boston: Houghton Mifflin, 1968. (A large and well-researched compendium on counseling topics.)

chapter
seven
Training
Supervisors
as Counselors

Any organization interested in altering the human talents and activities with which it is populated can choose from two alternative strategies: recruitment and training. A recruitment strategy emphasizes appointing as supervisors people who have predesignated characteristics, either by importing them from outside or by changing criteria for internal promotions. Contrastingly, a training strategy relies on transforming the attributes of personnel already incumbent in supervisory positions.

Obviously, these are not mutually incompatible strategies. They represent alternative variations in emphasis. Whenever an organization shifts the values it associates with different supervisory patterns, those shifts will tend to affect its recruitment and promotion policies, if only implicitly. Even when an organization has formally opted for a training strategy as its principal means of accomplishing change, a considerable portion of the long-term managerial change that may be attributed to training effects in reality is probably a result of changed recruitment practices that have gathered new people with the desired properties into the organization.

Recruitment strategies are feasible and useful (1) when individuals with appropriate characteristics are available and the organization has the capability of attracting them and (2) when organizational ends can be accomplished by redistributing existing personnel among the supervisory positions in the system. This last could occur via reassignments or modifications of criteria for promotion or both. It could be facilitated by suitable organization structural redesign. Wholesale importation of new personnel will usually yield more rapid results than other approaches to change, but ordinarily its costs in organizational disruption and human devastation will be such that it is best held to the minimum necessary, and that minimum should be carefully determined.

A training strategy, on the other hand, has humanity to recommend it. It endeavors to work with the personnel already in the system and to help them as well as the organization to progress. Training strategies can also capitalize on the commitments to and familiarity with the system that its existing personnel may have developed. Anyway, there may be no alternative to training if the conditions for recruitment cannot be met. Whether a recruitment or a training strategy will be cheaper in dollar terms will be highly variable and subject to case-by-case determination, as will be the issue of what combinations of each to employ in the setting of a particular organization and its goals. In any event, our concern here is with the implementation of training strategies.

Problems in Implementing Training Strategies

A major reason for dissatisfaction with the results of training is that training programs often yield meager changes in organizational practices.This is probably a consequence, for one thing, of failures to couple training with suitable policy determinations in the organization, the importance of which was stressed in Chapter 4. As a result of such neglect, the function trained is left unsupported by the system and may even conflict with other of its properties. For a trained function to be organizationally potent, it must be adapted to the actualities of life in the organization. Also, an appreciation of the function must be integrated into the thinking of the organization's management, and periodic evaluative-supportive supervisory follow-ups must be provided to build skills as well as attitudes. Thus, two equally important cornerstones of training exist: (1) satisfaction of the essentially technical requirements for training itself and (2) assurance of an appropriate organizational foundation for training efforts.

What does it take to develop practicable training programs that can teach work supervisors suitable counseling skills? This chapter represents some answers to those questions. Intended to further illuminate the relevance of counseling to organizational operation and development, the chapter draws on experiences with concrete training programs and reflects my beliefs about basic strategies for person-nel training and organizational development. It describes what I be-lieve is necessary to design a personally useful, organizationally im-pactful program of training. The chapter's focus is on counseling and the training of counseling skills, but the ideas offered are applica-ble to many different training and development activities.

Developing a Counseling Training Program

Encouraging a manager to adopt employee-centered goals and equipping him with employee-centered skills, including counseling, are major organizational moves directed toward the heart of organiza-tional functioning. Hence, they should hardly be undertaken in a perfunctory, even if well-intended, manner. Preparation, planning, and information are essential to development of a solid base from which to build a rational program designed to instill broad new skills previously unfamiliar to their users.

To be fully successful, a program of training must serve orienta-tional and motivational purposes as well as provide skills training. It must encourage participants to reflect critically on their approaches to management (read "leadership"). In addition, it must initiate exploration of practical techniques for the implementation of em-ployee-centered managerial perspectives and motivate on-the-job ap-plications of the program's ideas.

Meaningful training programs will be those designed not as an end but as a beginning. That is, they should be designed and conduct-ed with the assumption that follow-on activities will support, extend, develop, and update their perspectives. Recall the injunction cited earlier about the need to work at system maintenance. Valuable as they may be for certain purposes, off-site training, management re-treats, and other organizational development devices have limited utility as levers for organizational change. Since a training or develop-ment effort is in some way an attempt to change the way the work of an organization is performed, its continuity with the job must be established and provision must be made for resolving or accommo-dating impediments standing in the way of the implementation of training concepts. Moreover, training programs are materially en-hanced by being integrated into more comprehensive organizational development efforts involving direct and immediate on-the-job references. We have already discussed follow-on development concepts in Chapter 4, and, later in this present chapter, I will say more about their role in OD. For now, though, a summary restatement of my conception of counseling will help to get us started.

As I have described it, counseling is a problem-focused interaction process, having as its object learning, growth, and changed behavior. It is facilitated by the counselor's conveying genuine feelings of warmth, spontaneity, tolerance, respect, and sincerity. Devising practicable methods for the development of an appreciation of counseling by work supervisors and for building skill in its performance is the concern of the rest of this chapter.

Basic Technical Requirements for a Course of Counseling Training

The fundamental objective of a training program is arrangement of conditions such that some given content or contents can be acquired (learned) by some given target population. Obviously, a plurality of means will usually exist for achieving that objective. However, if economy, efficiency, impact, and retention are significant considerations, as they commonly are, training structures and procedures should be consistent both with known psychological principles of learning and with contemporary technical-procedural instructional expertise. Therefore, program formulation will wisely begin with a series of questions expressive of practical and technical problems, solutions to which constitute the requirements of effective program design. The first three questions have reference to general conditions of learning:

1. What is to be learned?
2. In what formats is material to be presented? (And what will be the role of the learner in relation to them?)
3. How will the learner be motivated?

When there is concern that a program yield on-the-job consequences, a fourth question arises:

4. How will the training program be related to the organizational environment and participant occupational functions? (This last question, of course, is familiar in professional counseling circles, but it is raised with surprising infrequency in work environments.)

Any answers to these questions, of course, will always express some kind of compromise, and more than one form of compromise might prove satisfactory. But, in any case, the particular answers chosen will define the core structure of a training or educational program. Therefore, planning such programs will profit from systematic attention to the more detailed considerations that follow.

WHAT IS TO BE LEARNED?

Definition of the content of a training program is divisible into three basic parts. First, it is necessary to identify the scope and dimensions of the body of knowledge to be learned. Second, it is necessary to segment this substantive body into meaningful teachable units that can form the building blocks of the program. Finally, these topical units must be organized into a coherent, integrated pattern, meaningful in itself and productive of the objectives of the program.

The definition of a subject matter should be based on empirical sources and other hard information relating to the organizations within which training is to be applied (a matter to which we shall return). But the definition will undoubtedly rely heavily, too, on ordinary consultation processes, on pre-existing relevant literatures, and on professional, technical, and theoretical knowledge or presumption—combined, I would hope, with heavy doses of common sense.

TRAINING STRUCTURES OR FORMATS

There are two aspects of training structures or formats: method and organization. Program contents entail presentation of material involving both concepts or ideas and skills (in varying combinations and amounts). It is necessary to assure that organization of this material is diversified, yet cumulative, with each part carrying its special load and building on, adding to, and supporting (rehearsing) what preceded it.

In addition, training should be planned with careful reference to organizational goals. Instructional staffs must be fully appreciative of a program's objectives and procedures. Furthermore, means must exist for controlling the process and the direction of the program as a whole. Briefing instructional staff and discussing program concepts are prerequisites to the first goal. I have found it helpful in actual training sessions to employ observers drawn from among training participants to critique the way things are going. It is also wise to distribute feedback sessions over a program's course.

Also of concern when structuring training, and a matter that relates as well to motivation, is the fundamental need to sustain interest and enhance impact. This need can be met in various ways, but I like to minimize stand-up lectures, to use audiovisual techniques, to vary methods of presentation, to encourage extensive participant involvement, to maintain program direction and progressive development of themes, and all the time to work hard to underscore job relevance.

Program formats, especially those having to do with skills practice, should be incremental and permit prompt feedback to trainees in order to facilitate shaping desired behavior. Group role-play methods, with emphasis on frequent brief performance by each individual and *immediate* feedback (critique of performance), are useful in this connection. Role-play programs may also be designed to focus selectively on particular counseling (or other training) issues, can culminate in final synthesis, and should strive to encourage participant exploration of new and alternative approaches to supervisory problems in the relatively safe environment of the training group.

Role-play scripts may be simple or detailed. They may also be projective in the sense that they require the role-player to draw on his own experiences and expertise in order to define for himself a situation described with a minimum of information, and then to improvise his performance. Projective role-plays presumably reveal more about a performer's modes of defining and handling supervisory situations, but they may or may not be useful instructional tools. Four examples of role-play scripts follow. The first two are simple and essentially projective. They deal with commonplace problems but leave matters largely to role-player improvisation. The third and especially the fourth cases go rather farther in providing background information and performance specification.*

CASE NO. 1

Background Information & Situation. It has been determined that a staffing imbalance exists in the company's

---

*A useful presentation of role-play and other related techniques can be found in Fordyce and Weil (1971).

Oshkosh plant due to the current workload. It is corporate policy to require the employee with the least seniority to move to another city. The employee with the least seniority is married, has five children, and has indicated indirectly that he is not mobile.

Role of the Supervisor. This employee has asked to see you to discuss the fairness of this policy and its application to him and to seek a revised decision.

CASE NO. 2

Background Information & Situation. One man has recently been promoted to a technical supervisory position. Twelve technicians are assigned to his group. One of them has the same education as the supervisor's and actually has had more experience, although he is only a bit older. He frequently disagrees with the supervisor on technical issues and has stated to others that he doubts the technical ability of his new supervisor.

Role of the Supervisor. You call this employee in to discuss his frequent disagreements. You are mainly concerned about the possible effect of this man's attitude on other members of your group.

Role of the Employee. You doubt your chief's technical ability and have so stated to other employees. Moreover, you resent having been passed over for promotion to a position for which you believe yourself qualified.

CASE NO. 3

Background Information & Situation. A middle manager, in the course of visiting one lower-level section head who doesn't report to the middle manager but whose section supplies work, has become aware of a problem that has upset many of the section head's people. It seems that one of the middle manager's staff assistants, a conscientious man many years his senior, explores the in-baskets of the personnel in this section.

Role of the Manager. You want to eliminate this irritant, so you call in the assistant.

Role of the Assistant. You know you will be receiving the work you have been checking up on in other sections, and you not only want to be aware of what's in the pipeline but want to make sure it's completed properly. Furthermore, you also know you have caught some errors before they became big problems.

CASE NO. 4

Background Information & Situation. This case is concerned with a civil servant who applied for entrance to a management-career-development program but was not selected. He received a letter advising him that his supervisor would discuss his rejected application and his future development with him if he requested an interview.

Employee. Mr. James is a Senior Technical Analyst GS–13. He has served in this position for several years, having previously served as a Technical Analyst GS–12. He has a firm grounding in management principles and is fully capable of analyzing the information provided him by a Junior Analyst. However, he has continually had difficulty in communicating his program recommendations to management personnel. Mr. James is 49 years of age, a college graduate with 12 years' experience in his government function and experience in private industry prior to that. Mr. James has been working for his present supervisor, Mr. Campbell, for the last two years. The personal relationship between Mr. James and Mr. Campbell is strained. However, Mr. Campbell has consistently rated Mr. James' overall performance as satisfactory. Mr. James achieved a high score on the test used as one of the selection factors.

Supervisor. Mr. Campbell is a Supervisory Analyst GS–14. He is 39 years of age, with 7 years' experience in the technical field. Prior to that he worked in private industry and with the military. Mr. Campbell applied for the executive-development program in his region and was accepted. In his relationship with Mr. James, he has had no reason to question the technical accuracy of Mr. James' work. However, he has had cause to be dissatisfied with the way Mr. James presents his findings, either in writing or orally. On several occasions, Mr. Campbell has tried to discuss the communications aspects of the job with Mr.

James but has had little or no success. Mr. Campbell feels that the development programs are an excellent way to begin shifting the emphasis from technical competence to supervisory potential when selections are made for supervisory positions. Within Mr. Campbell's office, this tends to be a minority point of view toward such programs. In supervising Mr. James, Mr. Campbell has chosen to rework portions of Mr. James' written reports to make them more palatable to the next audience.

Role of the Employee. You have been informed that it is your right to request an interview with your supervisor to discuss your nonselection for the career-development program. You do not feel that such a discussion will have any impact on your future in the organization, but you want a chance to confront your supervisor with what you very strongly believe to be an unjust situation. Since your test score was high, you believe you were not selected because you are over 45 and did not lie about how mobile you are. You feel that the career programs are a gift to the bright young man and fail to acknowledge the value of experience, technical competence, and mature judgment. In your discussion with Mr. Campbell, you will not be antagonistic enough to jeopardize your job, but you will not be concerned with how your behavior will affect your promotion opportunities. You are generally sour on your job and tend increasingly to look for your satisfactions outside of the work situation.

Role of the Supervisor. You are dreading the interview with Mr. James. You haven't been able to communicate effectively with him on anything but strictly technical subjects. You know that there is little or no mutual sympathy between the two of you and that Mr. James is probably very angry about his nonselection. You are aware that James' attitude can be a very disruptive force in your office. Furthermore, he is a capable Senior Analyst and does have some quasi-supervisory responsibilities.

The use of role-play techniques (or buzz-groups) is also a way of answering the question of the role to be played by the learner. It opts for active problem-solving as opposed to a passive role, appropriately I think, because this method shares control of the learning process with the learner and seems to yield superior results in both acquisition and retention, perhaps because of its motivating effects. Furthermore, role-play and group-oriented formats (which I favor) are well-adapted to skill training and provide a vehicle for drawing on the pooled wisdom of the participants as well as that of the teacher.

HOW SHALL LEARNERS BE MOTIVATED?

Numerous motivational sources can be drawn on or supplied in a training program. In a specific case, for example, one may already know several things from an organizational survey: for example, that program participants perceive counseling (or another training target) to be a legitimate, important function; that they relate it (even if uncertainly) to managerial/leadership/human-relations functions; and that they are concerned with the improvement of organizational management. One will still need to confront the problem, however, that supervisors typically tend to exaggerate their skills (after all, they *are* supervisors). Exposure to role-play problems and critique helps establish perspective and perhaps humility at the same time that it stimulates interest in further development. (At least it does when threat and evaluation anxiety are minimized in the group.)

Provision can be made, although it often isn't, for relating a program and the counseling function directly and meaningfully to the participants' organizational functions, to their legitimate interests in performance, and to general problems of management. Thereby, a rational frame of reference is provided for training while it is related explicitly to the participants' *individual* interests in job payoff. A motivationally effective technique for accomplishing this is to draw case material for discussion and to role-play from the immediate work context. That way, participants can deal with relatively familiar problem situations known to be of interest and concern. Some kind of pretraining organization survey can be an obvious assist in this connection.

An element of uncertainty can also be a useful motivator. It can be introduced, for instance, by such stratagems as failure to publish an agenda for the training program. (Instructors, of course, may and should possess an agenda.) Indeed, a useful procedure seems to be one in which a training program presents a high degree of structure from the standpoint of the instructional staff (they know what, when, how, and why they are doing things) but presents a distinctly unstructured appearance to its participants. As a result, they are required to grapple with uncertainty, to come up with their own answers to important questions of personal relevance, and to accept responsibility for their activities all the while they are supplied with ideas and information and are guided through a purposeful progression of experiences.

Mild anxiety (anxiety can be a salutary motivator when kept mild) can be induced by the context and nature of the program itself, by the implicit pressures of the program schedule, by the role-play technique, and, of course, by critique. Careful management of anxiety must be provided, however, principally by maintenance of a generally nonpunitive climate, by feedback discussion sessions, by reward for performance change (responsibility for which must fall to the group leader), and by staff moderation and good judgment. Brutality, even to people who have it coming, has no place in education, and hiding it behind euphemistic labels like "confrontation" changes nothing.

THE TRAINER'S PART IN MANAGING ROLE-PLAYING

Effective use of role-play methods is a delicate process. So much involves intangibles: when to stop a role-play; when or whether to switch roles; how to work with "true believers"; judging when issues are "too close to home" to be explored further; acknowledging the many individualistic ways that counseling can be conducted; deciding when to state a firm position about substance or method and when to back off to leave room for others. These intangibles are complicated further by the fact that the trainer's own experience, personality, and relationship to the group will influence how he works.

It is possible, nevertheless, to offer some general recommendations that can help make for more successful use of role-play methods. Listed below are two classes of desired behavior—one to be evidenced by the group of colleagues critiquing the role-play and one by the trainer working with the group. These can serve as loose guidelines for managing the several aspects of purposeful role-play.

1. *Group.* The group's comments are specific and illustrative. Broad generalizations are used infrequently, and critique does not wander into reminiscences or irrelevancies.

Trainer. The trainer sets an example of specificity and pertinence with his own comments, follows up on the discussion of an exchange, and draws analogies to other similar behavior in this and other role-plays. He helps the group maintain focus on the issues at hand and strives to avoid digressions that center on the role-players' acting abilities.

2. *Group.* The group appears to operate independently. It moves on with the critique with a minimum of outside guidance. On occasion, however, the members ask for the trainer's opinion.

Trainer. The trainer participates in the critique to help the group move forward, not just to demonstrate his own virtuosity. He does not, however, hide his light under a bushel; he takes a stand when he has something to contribute that can help the group or when the group's progress would be hindered if he remained passive.

3. *Group.* The members of the group demonstrate an understanding of the role-players' reactions to their critiques by being as personally nonjudgmental in their comments as possible. That is, they stress the performance, not the performer.

Trainer. The trainer sets an example of nonjudgmental critique. He encourages acknowledgment of the difficulties and threatening aspects of role-play exposure. He assures comment on positive aspects of performance.

4. *Group.* The group is willing to be critical, to make negative comments about the role-play (not about the role-player). They do not shy away from issues because they may be unpleasant or because of the status of the performer.

Trainer. The trainer sets an example of facing unpleasant issues if this is necessary. As needed, the instructor acts to temper or objectify role-players' emotional responses to negative criticism. He tries to orient role-play evaluations around the objectives the performers were trying to achieve.

5. *Group.* The group acknowledges the wide range of effective counseling behavior. Critiques are offered with an understanding of individualistic approaches.

Trainer. The trainer works with players and critiquers to get an understanding of the varied behavior appropriate in counseling. He reacts to the here-and-now, not to stereotypes of the good counselor and counselee. He encourages experimentation with other than habitual ways of handling supervisory problems.

6. *Group.* The group shows interest in the different counseling approaches used and in substantive or content questions—for example, the counseling process and the content of the session, apart from the particular technique used.

   Trainer. The trainer directs attention to the counseling process and the relevant subject-matter questions in the counseling session. He discourages the group from critiquing the content of the role-play—that is, how accurate it might be as a mirror of organizational reality. (If the contents of role-plays have been carefully chosen, little of this should be necessary.)

7. *Group.* The group demonstrates sensitivity to the cues the role-players give about the way they feel during the role-play. The group uses this perception to help the players better understand their performance and motivation.

   Trainer. The trainer helps the group learn how to demonstrate sensitivity by identifying and working with cues he has observed.

8. *Group.* The group is able to react to emotionality in the role-play and accept emotional reactions in the critique. The group atmosphere is neither emotionally flat nor highly charged and is fundamentally supportive.

   Trainer. The trainer demonstrates through his own example that he considers emotion an integral part of interpersonal relationships, neither to be overly feared nor held in awe.

What runs through all these recommendations is the idea that the counseling trainer should be practicing what he preaches, demonstrating in each situation the merit of the perspective. Essential to this and to participant motivation both for training and subsequent practice is a nonpunitive, help-oriented, interpersonal training climate.

Maintaining (within limits and when possible) a flexible posture toward program design, content, and procedure, and allowing these to shift or change somewhat in response to process feedback as well as emerging participant needs and interests, can also augment motivation. By allowing for operational flexibility, the motivating consequences of shared control over program features may be engaged.

Finally, discipline from the framework of a well-designed and well-executed program serves to focus motivation on activities productive of the program's objectives instead of on incidentals or irrelevancies.

THE PROBLEM OF ORGANIZATIONAL IMPACT

Some program strategies contributing to achievement of organizational impact have already been described—for example, those having to do with rendering a program job-relevant. In addition, provision may be made at the end of training for consideration of requirements and responsibilities for and barriers against on-the-job implementation of newly trained skills and concepts.

Barriers to the implementation of training. Training is only as good as its implementation. If the functions being trained can't or won't be used, even the best instructional program is an organizationally idle exercise.

It is best to try to identify in advance what some of the impediments to use of the training might be, in the hope that knowing them will make possible their elimination or at least amelioration. Typically, I have included in counseling training programs, as the last item on the agenda, group discussion of barriers to implementation. From the results of those discussions, I can distill a sort of laundry list of commonly perceived barriers to on-the-job counseling. I offer that five-part list for your review and reflection.

1. *Employee Receptivity to Counseling*
   —Reluctance of employees to "level" (deficiencies of employee trust in the good will of their superiors).
2. *Supervisor/Manager Motivation*
   —Lack of suitable orientation toward employees.
   —Failure to plan time so as to make counseling feasible.
   —Prejudices and conflicts of interest.
   —Unwillingness to risk involvements in human relationships.
   —Reluctance to handle tough problems (especially emotion-laden ones).
3. *Ownership of Requisite Skill*
   —Knowledge of how to plan work and time.
   —Uncertainties about working with groups.
   —Lack of knowledge of specific counseling techniques.

4. *Structure, Character, and Organization of the Work Environment*
   —Inadequate physical facilities (a lack of privacy).
   —Lack of time (too much pressure from other duties, especially administrative tasks, paper work, red tape).
   —Poor communications.
   —Inadequate planning on the part of management (failure to include supervisors in the planning process).
   —Organizational structures that tend to by-pass supervisors, reducing their apparent influence and prestige and removing incentives for performance.

5. *Management Policies*
   —Uncertainties about the actual existence of a supportive managerial climate.
   —Inability of lower-level supervisors to influence higher-level management decisions.
   —Lack of authority and autonomy on the part of supervisors to make and implement decisions and/or to delegate work and authority.
   —Barriers posed by organizational policies and practices that both consume time and constrain attitudes commensurate with employee-centered concepts of management.
   —Failures to inform supervisors and other management about relevant events within the system (for example, reasons for nonselections of personnel under their supervision for management-development career programs).

How meaningful, important, or legitimate these perceived barriers may be to the implementation of training in a particular organization I cannot say. However, they were identified as impediments in one or another setting and so must be regarded as real possibilities. Beyond commending them to the attention of management, though, there is little more to say except to propose consideration of whether such impediments (and others) exist in one's own organization and to suggest their elimination if maximum program impact is desired.

The basic problem here is motivating and subsequently sustaining and rewarding performance *on the job*, where it counts. There must be real payoff to the supervisor, resulting from organizational accommodation, support, and help. Support and help can come in the form of follow-on phasing of a project, including activities such as discussion groups, seminars, and skills training, distributed at intervals through time and conducted wholly on the job during the regular work day.

POSTTRAINING FOLLOW-ON

A follow-on plan would have the intended consequence of making possible diagnosis and treatment of barriers to implementation of training and of opening internal lines of communication potentially productive on other counts. Furthermore, it would actualize the theoretical job-relevance of training and make on-the-job supervision and skill development feasible. Finally, it has the technical virtue of distributing practice, thereby helping to improve retention.

Learning by doing. Critical to the full development of counseling or any other supervisory skill is the opportunity to practice it in the real world, on the job. A man will learn from the mistakes and the successes he experiences while trying to put into practice ideas and methods he may glean from various sources. This process will, however, be both facilitated and better controlled if it is linked with organizational provisions for review, critique, and forward planning of performance. As someone else has said, it is the difference between unguided and guided learning.

Concerning the matter of change, a couple of additional observations are in order, especially as regards the difficult transformation of work-centered, status-conscious supervisors into people-oriented, democratic ones.

In the first place, this transformation is a very hard thing to accomplish. A great change is asked of a man—a change freighted with implicit criticism of his past performance, uncertainty, and risk. To achieve it, a manager may need a great deal of encouragement and support, and that depends on training follow-on. Any time management personnel are exploring new concepts and methods, they need help and heartening lest they slip back into the comfortably familiar channels of habitual practices. It is well to remember that individual people, like complex organizations, are systems of order. They do not ordinarily change very readily (although they sometimes do so explosively).

Second, protestations to the contrary notwithstanding, in many organizations there still exist very narrow conceptions of supervisory roles—conceptions that allow little room for so-called people functions. These bents of thought often are little affected by training or managerial exhortation. An opportunity for supervisory confrontation of them might be necessary. One interesting way to help accomplish that is via the participation of nonsupervisory employees in training programs and in serious workshop discussion sessions relative to supervisory roles and responsibilities. I have found it useful, for example, to include one or more union representatives in management-training programs.

Summarizing what has been said to this point is the following list of eight technical requirements that any specific training program must be designed to satisfy if it is to qualify as an optimal learning experience:

1. It must specify what is to be learned.
2. It must include means to motivate learning.
3. It must provide a meaningful, individually relevant framework for learning and an opportunity for give-and-take critique of individual and organizational performance.
4. It must provide for the reinforcement and incremental shaping of behavior.
5. It must provide continuing knowledge of results (feedback) over its course.
6. It must provide an active, problem-solving role for the learner.
7. It should distribute skills practice through time, rather than in a mass all at once.
8. It should concern itself with problems of gaining subsequent organizational impact and afford a rewarding group-based experience within the organizational context.

Organizational Bases for a Course of Counseling Training

Since training of the sort that concerns us here is always conducted in a particular organizational context, its targets, strategies, and tactics need to be selected and formulated with reference to that context. It is my conviction that, while efforts to humanize organizations are laudable and attempts to improve supervisory performance desirable, the responsible addition to the supervisor's role of a skill such as counseling must be done according to a coherent plan rooted in detailed, relevant information about the organizational and human context into which the skill is to be introduced. I believe, in short, that supervisory skills are relative not only to the problems of supervision in a given organization but also to the goals of that organization and to its social-psychological climate. Therefore, this information should be known in some detail in order that changes in organizational practice can be tailored to achieve maximum effect.

Most especially, the new role must be seen in the clear light of the old role. Anyone planning a training and development program needs to know to what extent and in what areas both supervisor and subordinate are or are not prepared to accept the modified role. A program planner needs to understand what the total set of influences molding the definition of roles in the system is. Finally, some attempt needs to be made to define precisely and in organizationally relevant terms the nature of the new skills to be distributed to the supervisor. It is basic to the success of any training or development program that its techniques be adapted to the nature, the needs, values, and interests of both those who experience training and those with whom the newly learned skills will be used; and it is just as basic that impediments to training and subsequent use of it be foreseen wherever they are capable of being foreseen. In other words, training-program designs should reflect organizational reality as well as satisfy technical requirements for learning. At minimum, this will necessitate that planners or trainers (1) specify training needs, (2) identify relevant organizational properties that can be taken for granted as far as a particular development program is concerned, (3) formulate policy guidelines for program content, and (4) consider ways to evaluate training.

THE NEED FOR TRAINING

Elementary as it seems, it nevertheless bears stating that a need for training (at least of the kind discussed here) should be established before actual training is undertaken. Training efforts should not degenerate into a kind of organizational "keeping up with the Jones's" or be motivated by the notion that "it can't hurt." Maybe it can. Once a genuine need is documented, attention can turn to stating the forms that training or other efforts might take. Determination of training needs, both individual and collective, can use a variety of inputs, including implications of existing system-development programs, the aspirations and experience of management, and so on. However, hard empirical documentation is crucial to determining actual training needs. Some form of organizational survey is the only device that can effectively satisfy that need. Furthermore, survey data can be integrated into the training on more general OD programs, as I suggested earlier. Survey feedback and survey-guided development, for example, are terms describing general strategies for the planned review of survey-derived information about organizational phenomena as a means of facilitating change (see Bowers & Franklin, 1972).

WHAT CAN BE TAKEN FOR GRANTED

Ordinarily, not every aspect of an organization requires renovation. It will, therefore, be useful to identify already satisfactory organizational properties that may be reasonably disregarded in the design of a training program.

By way of illustration: before designing counseling-training programs (or other change-oriented action), I try to determine whether those who are to participate in training are already disposed toward change, even if they may be unenthusiastic about it. Most importantly, management dispositions must be consistent with the training or development directions that seem otherwise appropriate. In this way, at least in principle, management support for the training can be expected. What should be avoided (or anticipated as a barrier to the use of training) is the following kind of situation, which was cited by one supervisor as the reason for his failure to do much counseling:

> Supervisors don't really have enough time. We've had to give priority to getting the work out. On the basis of management policies you have to decide which things are most important, and counseling isn't one of them. I've yet to fill out a report on how much counseling I've done this week, but I fill out a lot on production, schedules, and costs.

On another level, before such efforts as counseling training are undertaken, it seems to me that a generally sound interpersonal situation must exist in an organization and that employees must be prepared to accept a larger motivational and human-relations role on the part of their supervisors. It can only be futile to strive for supervisory role change when the organizational context is inhospitable to the changed role. Of course, attempts at changing that context are not precluded, but they must take forms different from the counseling training itself.

PROGRAM CONTENT

The issue of what a program of training should include and how it should be put together is, of course, a fundamental one. In dealing with the issue, data generated from organizational surveys are invaluable, even if they cannot be absolutely decisive. They can inform and support it, but statistics cannot substitute for wise judgment. Nor can they answer all questions pertaining to program form and substance. Content decisions, like most others, depend on numerous conceptual, procedural, and other considerations apart from direct empirical benchmarks.

Regarding content, one thing seems evident from my experience: the particulars of counseling training need to be conceptualized in relation to an across-the-board approach to management and supervision. Specific technical and interpersonal skills are of course relevant to the development of managerial proficiency. However, concrete operational skills can achieve maximum impact only within a more comprehensive philosophical frame of reference that gives them point and broader generality. Interpersonally oriented training programs are needed that are capable of expanding supervisors' awareness of their role—programs that can extend the concept of supervision to include larger leadership burdens. Managerial responsibilities for motivating employee membership and performance within the organization are basic to this envisaged role, as are concerns with the guidance and career development of subordinates. Counseling is cogent to these tasks.

Communication and cultivation of interpersonal skills productive of higher levels of mutual understanding and trust within an organization will be obvious touchstones of counseling training. Supervisory and managerial personnel can be helped to develop a wider sense of responsibility to the organization, to their subordinates, and to themselves, along with a conviction of the productive utility of employee- centered, participative, and generalized styles of supervision. More mutuality and less paternalism can be taken as bedrock objectives of development and training processes.

EVALUATING TRAINING

Achieving meaningful evaluation of the results of training is a perplexing problem that has long bedeviled educators and professional trainers. And the difficulties increase with the complexity of the functions being learned and with the scope of the curriculum. In other words, whenever a program of training is functionally complex and broad of scope, its results are very hard to appraise.

One important issue in evaluation has to do with its timing. Oftentimes the interval allowed between training and test is too short for training effects to have germinated. In complex systems, apparent lack of change in the short term does not assure a lack over the long term. And quite apart from this either-or effect, it is also possible for short-term system changes to fail to correlate with long-term modifications or even for the two to be negatively related. For example, something that looked good right after its organizational introduction might look terrible after its extended system-wide reverberations are experienced. As a result, short-run evaluations may be highly uncertain predictors of long-run consequences.

The obvious methodological solution to this problem is to conduct strategically spaced follow-up evaluations. However, this is a matter of strategy. It does not speak to the issues of tactics or of the exact procedures by which evaluation may be conducted. Here there seem to be several traditional alternatives.

The testimonial. One approach to evaluation, hallowed by tradition if by little less, has been the solicitation of testimonials from program participants, chiefly from its staff. This is sometimes a useful procedure. But the evaluations it yields have an unhappy way of being self-congratulatory, self-serving declarations. The method is of dubious validity; it should be used sparingly and certainly advisedly.

The posttraining questionnaire. A somewhat more satisfactory method of assessment is to administer a questionnaire of some kind to the training program's students. This method has the sturdy virtue of objectivity and the further advantage of being addressed to a more relevant target, but it has serious limitations that circumscribe its value.

Quite aside from its being a distinctly short-run procedure, the posttraining questionnaire measures mainly immediate reactions to the training program as such. It does not necessarily reveal anything about the program's effects on the functions ostensibly being trained. Still, it can be a valuable device when used with healthy respect for its limitations.

The training pre- and posttest. The most satisfactory method for assessing training effects is direct and controlled measurement of the functions being trained. It is also the most laborious, the most costly, and the most difficult technically.

Its preferred form includes, in addition to objective measurement, pretraining and posttraining tests and the use of comparable but nontrained control groups. This form permits an appraisal of change and also allows for determination of the degree to which change can be attributed expressly to training.

TRAINING PROGRAMS AND PROFESSIONAL CONSULTANTS

I shall not debate the categorical desirability of retaining outside consultants. Presumably, they possess knowledge and expertise unavailable within the system or else a latitude for operation impossible for members of the organization that justifies their retention.

Nor shall I argue the merits of developing suitable in-house capabilities. That is a goal any sensible person must concede in principle.

What is at issue is how best to use consultants and when. I have devoted some attention to the subject in Chapter 4, but I do have two immediately pertinent additional thoughts in the matter:

1. Interpersonal processes like counseling involve skills. The tradition (if it is a tradition) of entrusting the training of those skills wholly to instructors themselves possessing only marginal competence is absurd and grossly unfair to the instructors no less than it is to the student. I am therefore sympathetic with the plaint of trainees who observe that, being blind themselves, they would prefer not always to be led by other blind men or even by the partially sighted. *Skills should be trained in close consultation with persons who have them.*

2. My second thought is different. In an in-house training effort, the actual employment of an outside consultant, because of his status and nominal expertise, sometimes tends to have disruptive effects. It undermines the position of the in-house staff and creates a condition in which people may sit around waiting for the "doctor" to come tell them what to do and how to do it. This damps a program's spontaneity and misdirects its focus, causing an *overdependence* on the skills of the consultant. For this reason, programs that intend to operate with mainly in-house personnel might be better advised to operate entirely with in-house personnel and to use the consultant to help prepare them, the program, and its evaluation.

A Counseling Training Prototype

In this chapter we have discussed training and development chiefly in relation to stylistic objectives associated with counseling functions. None of these, as I have commented, is inconsistent with fostering the acquisition of specific, concrete skills facilitative of effective supervision. Development of such skills in a framework of organizational concern with production, performance, and efficient use of time seems a perfectly reasonable training objective. Indeed, counseling consists operationally of an array of familiar skills (listening, communication artistry, and so on) integrated around an attitude or a point of view: the counseling perspective.

Thus, any program of counseling training will be best regarded as an initial step in a development process. It ought to focus on a conception of counseling as an approach to work supervision, jointly stressing attributes of leadership and sensitivity to human needs. Fostering attention to the importance of communication processes in organizational operation must be central to such a program, just as the development of interpersonal skills must be helpful in building understanding, trust, motivation, and wider system participation and involvement.

Such a program should also contribute to integration of management echelons, help inculcate managerial perspectives, and at least begin to build bridges between skills training and on-the-job performance requirements. In the end, its consequences must be substantial enlargement of supervisory and managerial roles and responsibilities and widespread enhancement of the mental-hygienic environment of work.

Finally, to exemplify concretely the training concepts set forth in this chapter, it may be instructive to describe briefly what an actual training effort might look like.

Programmatically stated, what I am endeavoring to do is not only to design an isolated training course but to develop a model program for interconnecting skills training, policy formulation, and broad-scale organizational change. The program is oriented toward the future as well as toward past conditions of the organization and is capable of integration with other development activities.

The program model described here is an intensive, off-site experience, intended for implementation on a small-group basis with any and all levels of management personnel, either separately or intermixed. The program could include trainees and would not necessarily exclude nonmanagement personnel. As a learning experience, the program strives to satisfy the eight technical training requirements described earlier.

Immediately prior to implementation of the training program, a detailed briefing session for its instructor staff (consultants or in-house) should be conducted, in order to familiarize them thoroughly with the schedule, materials, and rationale for the program and to consider particular instructional techniques. This session may or may not be enunciated as a formal program component. But such a briefing is essential in order to enable the instructional staff to adapt to needs and exigencies that arise during training without straying from the thrust and spirit of the program's conceptualization.

The program outlined has basic-skills training as its principal operational purpose, but it is more appropriately regarded as orientational and motivational. Although capable of standing on its own, the program's impact would be amplified if its design were fleshed out and its conduct consistent with an assumption of follow-on activities to support, extend, and develop its perspectives.

To develop a cogent and practical short course of counseling training consistent with theoretical requirements for learning, a program of six topical content components may be planned, and specific techniques may be selected for their presentation. I shall do no more than outline them here. The components selected define the specific program objectives. The techniques, when combined with individual instructor strategies, define the program's methodology. In sequential order, the constituents of a hypothetical counseling-training program might be as follows.*

MODERN CONCEPTS OF MANAGEMENT

This component relates the program's content to larger issues of leadership and management strategies and tactics. It thereby provides a fundamental yet broad-gauge frame of reference within which the program as a whole can be rationalized. In practice, this might consist of short factual presentations (such as a lecturette or a film) of concepts and even data linking employee-centered leadership practices with the system concept, motivation, morale, and productivity.

Documenting the organizational effectiveness of employee-centered approaches to leadership is important in order to establish

---

*The remainder of this chapter is based on an article by myself and Cary M. Lichtman entitled "A Prototype Program for Training Work Supervisors as Employee Counselors," *Training and Development Journal*, 1970, **24**(8), 26–32.

the legitimacy of the program and stimulate interest in development. By plain implication, leadership becomes the central focus of the program.

CONNECTING LEADERSHIP THEORY TO THE JOB CONTEXT

The previous activity undertook to offer a coherent, theoretical, and general empirical basis for the program's orientation and message. Its broad purpose was to stimulate thought about how the ideas and information presented relate to the participants' actual job context. In practice, I have generally employed buzz-group discussions of the problems and responsibilities of management.

Groups can profitably specialize during such discussion, with different ones dealing, say, with management's responsibility to the organization, to subordinates, to the public, and to self. Groups can ordinarily be allowed relative freedom in deciding on an approach to their problem, but the instructor-leader must retain responsibility for maintaining focus on the issue. Each group should appoint a *recorder* (not the instructor-leader), who will maintain a record of the group's conclusions and report these in a feedback session.

In addition, the buzz-group may nominate one member to serve *for that session only* as an *observer*. This observer can stand apart, keep notes, and feed back his impressions of the group's progress and processes at selected intervals. No observer should serve for more than a single session, since such a role obviously precludes his participation in the program. (The same holds for recorders.)

The observer can make an important contribution to the success of a training program. His responsibility is to help the group stay on course and progress efficiently toward its objectives. He does not participate directly in the group processes but carefully observes, records notes, and evaluates the group's activities, diagnosing difficulties and supplying information to the group about its performance. In addition, he may be asked to share his judgments with the assembled group. Here are some basic questions for an observer to ask about the group's activities: Do we have a direction toward a goal? How successful have we been in keeping oriented in that direction, staying on the subject, not wandering off course? How are we progressing? Are we moving forward at a reasonable rate or have we bogged down? Are we applying our full group potential? Is everyone contributing? What barriers to participation seem to exist? What things made it easy or hard to participate in the discussion? Are we improving in our ability to work together more effectively? Are there any facts or ideas the group needs?

COUNSELING AS AN APPROACH TO MANAGEMENT

The first two program elements establish a rational frame of reference and should initiate exploration of the program's relevance to the job, but only in an abstract, intellectual way. How managerial responsibilities can actually be implemented within an employee-centered framework still has to be concretely realized.

To introduce this subject, I have regularly made use of discussions of pretraining readings (holding these to a minimum, though) and films that point up case-oriented problems and functions of leadership, supervision, understanding, human relations, and communications. These discussions serve as meaningful and stimulating lead-ins to consideration of counseling as a way of implementing their perspectives.

In this program phase, it must be the responsibility of the instructors to introduce consideration of the relevance to management of counseling perspectives. Discussion might be led first into general examination of the nature of counseling (touching on communication, participation, human needs, and so on). Then, later, counseling's special relevance to solution of supervisory problems can be addressed. To aid and enhance this process, some brief pretraining informational reading about concepts of counseling is useful (such as Chapters 5 and 6 in this book).

As in any other group session, a process observer should be named, because this kind of feedback, in all forms, is most helpful in keeping training on the track.

COUNSELING KEYSTONES

At this point, the program moves to more detailed analysis of the counseling concept and its techniques. At specific issue is the fundamental significance of the supervisory relationship in organizational performance. Successive consideration of the counseling keystones discussed in Chapter 6 can be introduced at this point.

While examining these keystones, the program can enter a skill-training phase wherein some sharpening of suitable technique is sought, perhaps via role-play methods. It is worth noting, however, that at this early time I have usually avoided specific instruction in "how to do it," preferring to allow participants to grapple with the concepts, adapt methods to their own personal styles, and rely on group critique to shape performance.

I have customarily begun consideration of the counseling keystones with the problem of listening. As a lead-in to exploration of this issue, I have ordinarily used a film about listening that can be shown after a short introduction. Following the film (or some other suitable beginning), I immediately break groups out for role-play sessions, during which it is the responsibility of the instructor to sustain special focus on the listening problem in the critique of role-play.

Each group should again select an *observer*. I have generally encouraged the instructor-leader to appoint role-players according to his or her own judgment of the people and circumstances in the group. However, I have stipulated that the critique-feedback of role-plays be led in such fashion as to help the group keep especially in mind the particular counseling issue at hand (for example, listening) rather than how things turned out; consideration of that larger problem should be a later program component. The instructor can usually begin discussion-critique with the supervisor role-player, by asking for his evaluation of his own performance. He then can turn to group discussion by inquiring, for example, about whether the other role-player felt understood.

In addition to maintaining focus, the instructor must endeavor to facilitate a supportive, nonpunitive climate (ensuring reward for the role-player) and try to guarantee that observers giving either especially high or low marks to the role-play describe their reactions. I have used various familiar devices—such as role reversal, asking for repetition of what has been said, and so on—to test understanding (and other things, too) in the role-play.

Preparation time for the role-playing should be held to an absolute minimum. I have used scripts dealing with routine matters and intended to be essentially projective. Typically at this point in training, I plan for role-plays and feedback periods to last no more than 10 to 15 minutes. The aspiration is to complete about three role-plays per hour. Even more may be completed, so plainly a sufficient number of cases needs to be provided for the instructor's use.

Lead-ins to other keystones and handling of role-plays can be essentially similar to what has just been described. (Consideration might also be given to using various demonstrations, such as the Leavitt demonstration of one-way versus two-way communication [Leavitt, 1964].) As each of the keystones is dealt with in its turn, the focus in role-play and critique shifts to the particular issue involved (for example, from listening to two-way communication).

PROBLEMS IN COUNSELING

In the preceding activities, counseling and skill training proceeded on a largely segmental basis, concentrating on each of the keystones one at a time. However, this fifth phase of the program tries to encourage synthesis. It also emphasizes evaluation of counseling outcomes on the basis of larger results rather than on the implementation of specific techniques. As lead-ins to this activity, buzz-group discussions can be pointed toward formulation of a working concept of counseling consistent with the concepts and activities experienced in the program and suitable to real-world organizational use. Recorders feed back the results of small-group discussions at a subsequent assembled session oriented toward synthesizing and integrating their separately developed ideas. Furthermore, I have used "meatier" role-plays in this phase—role-plays having both immediate relationship relevance and also broader implications for organizational policy.

I usually select three general issues for emphasis in these role-plays: dealing with the disgruntled employee, counseling with incomplete information, and motivating improved performance on the part of already satisfactory personnel.

Role-play procedures in this phase should allow more preparation time and fuller discussion, centering on larger strategies and outcomes. At this point, too, role-plays should be longer and oriented toward solution. Moreover, a staff (or a filmed) demonstration of counseling technique might precede role-playing, and the availability of videotape equipment can be a real boon to performance review (as it can during the previous phase, too).

BARRIERS TO IMPLEMENTATION OF TRAINING

Finally I turn to assembled group discussion of why the training and/or its perspectives may not be implemented on the job. (Ideally, these sessions should be attended by organizational top management.) Here one may try to stimulate discussion of management policies, production requirements, availability of time, and management-supervisor relations.

During such sessions, pertinent results from any attitude or organizational surveys can be fed back, and discussion of their implications can be encouraged, perhaps beginning in buzz-groups and moving to an assembled session. (This feedback can also sometimes be an effective tactic during the second and third phases of the training.) What one can strive to accomplish in these sessions is to direct training toward the job context, to motivate performance, to anticipate and expose impediments to implementation, and to link the counseling function with organizational policies and structures. Moreover, sharing of individual and general managerial responsibility for organizational development can be underscored.

PROGRAM TERMINATION

In an attempt to communicate the on-going continuity of training, development, and organizational activity, I have often designed programs without formal conclusions or a wrap-up. The purpose of this stratagem is to convey a sense of future expectation that is consistent with the forward-looking emphases of the model.

DURATION OF TRAINING

Excluding time for preparation and any follow-on activities, I have found it possible to complete a course of training comfortably in 23 to 24 hours, although I have done it less comfortably in less time. Obviously, more time could be used to good advantage; but time is commonly a rare commodity and between a trade-off of more training time for less follow-on activity and the reverse, I would unhesitatingly choose to sacrifice training for follow-on.

Just as many different schedules are possible, so are a large number of thematic and design variations possible on the basic concept of the model program outlined. By the same token, countless procedural variations can be introduced, some of which I have noted, others of which can be left to the ingenuity of program administrators. I would only comment that the one crucial requirement of an instructor in any program is that he maintain the task focus of each session. He must restrain quibbling about the content of roles and encourage experimentation. Fulfilling that responsibility simply depends on the instructor-leader knowing what he is about, both conceptually and procedurally.

References

Bowers, D. G., & Franklin, J. L. Survey-guided development. *Journal of Contemporary Business*, 1972, **1**, 43–57.

Fordyce, J. K., & Weil, R. *Managing with people*. Reading, Mass.: Addison-Wesley, 1971.

Hunt, R. G., & Lichtman, C. M. A prototype program for training work supervisors as employee counselors. *Training and Development Journal*, 1970, **24**, 26–36.

Hunt, R. G., & Lichtman, C. M. Pre-test influences in evaluating the organizational effects of a supervisory counseling training program. *Journal of Applied Behavioral Science*, **8**(4), 1972.

Leavitt, H. J. *Managerial psychology*. (Rev. ed.) Chicago: University of Chicago Press, 1964.

Recommended Readings

Bass, B. M. & Vaughan, J. A. *Training in industry: The management of learning*. Monterey, Calif.: Brooks/Cole, 1966. (A satisfactory, comprehensive discussion of principles and methods of training, along with techniques for their evaluation.)

Dunnette, M. D., & Kirchener, W. K. *Psychology applied to industry*. New York: Appleton-Century-Crofts, 1965. (Contains a good brief outline of survey methods.)

Seiler, J. A. *Systems analysis in organizational behavior*. Homewood, Ill.: Richard D. Irwin, 1967. (For helpful treatments of approaches to diagnosing training needs.)

chapter eight

Extensions of the Counseling Concept

The image of counseling and supervision projected so far in this book has been pretty much a traditional one, consisting essentially of one person talking with another about things of mutual interest. That image and the philosophical precepts I have gathered around it will remain basic, but now we turn to some alternative ways of carrying out supervisory counseling. In addition to touching on concepts of nondirective counseling, this chapter reviews group approaches to counseling and supervision and discusses further the idea of focusing supervision on explicit behavioral targets. In this latter connection, the chapter contains an overview of modern behavior-change principles and methods.

In a previous chapter, I talked about barriers to implementation of managerial counseling skills. These barriers, I suggested, are to be found in prevailing styles of management, organizational customs, or in managers' personal concerns about their status prerogatives. Sometimes barriers may also be found in the attitudes or aptitudes of supervisors or in the personal characteristics of employees, a subject to which I shall return shortly. Commonly though, barriers will lurk mainly in the policies, practices, and structures of organizations. Often hard to identify and frequently resistive to change, these organizational properties are nevertheless discoverable and subject to modification. Some general approaches to that have been outlined earlier in the review of the properties of organizational systems and still more directly in my presentations of organic-development concepts and counseling training methods. Implicit in the concept of organic development is the idea that good, innovative management methods will have a better chance of taking root and flourishing if they are realistically adapted to existing organizational environments. Let's take a fundamental example.

If there is one thing most managers don't have a lot of it's time. Working days are typically crowded; events pile on events; the unplanned and unexpected are routine. Hurried, harried, and worried, the manager often feels his schedules slipping out of hand and, with them, his ability to control his own activities (to say nothing of his temper). Then he is advised: "Counsel your employees; get to know your people and their needs and àspirations so that you may individualize supervision; take the time to listen, understand, and talk with your people." But where in hell does the time come from? We have already heard one supervisor's answer in Chapter 7. In any one day, there are only so many hours, and there just is no way to get more time than there is.

So much is sure; but there does exist the possibility of using the time that is available differently. Another manager, for example, describing his own primary development needs, put this notation close to the top of his list: "increased ability to plan and organize—time pressures are too great—need training in how best to use time, establishing priorities, and the like." Enter the efficiency expert.

Everybody knows that time can be functionally increased by organizing it more effectively, by introducing certain time-saving management systems, or by staff delegations. Even quick examinations of work settings often reveal obvious possibilities for simple ways of effecting significant management time savings. (Management consultants, wise to the ways of inspiring confidence in their acumen, have long since learned places to look first.) However, one organization I studied regularly lost upwards of one working hour each day from each first-line supervisor as a result of the average time required to wade through the daily flood of office memoranda. One way to effect time savings in many such work situations is to identify and put a leash on the "memo freaks" (commonly found with increasing density as one ascends toward the management summit). In the particular office cited, it wasn't so simple, however; most of the memos were necessary. Time savings can still be effected in such situations; the length of memos might be reduced (by edict?), their form could be simplified (there are consultants for that, too), or one might try increasing supervisors' information-processing capabilities. (A course in speedreading for supervisors, for example, if it could reduce memo-processing time by 20%, could allow discovery of as much as 76 extra working hours per year per supervisor.) But once the time has been found, beware the Parkinsonian principle that work expands to fill the time available for it. The trick is to fill any time gained with organizationally desirable activities—counseling, for example.

Thus there are ways supervisory time may be "found." But assuming that managers do anything of substance with their time, the number of hours to be found this way will probably not be great. Seventy-some hours a year, after all, is not exactly a bonanza. Therefore, somehow spreading managerial time more effectively has to be an alluring prospect.

Mental-health practitioners and professional counselors face a very similar problem and have developed more than a few procedural innovations for dealing with it. One of these, an early one, was group psychotherapy and counseling. It was at least partly premised on the idea that therapists could better provide service to patients by abandoning the traditional one-to-one model of practice for a one-to-several (or even one-to-many) variation. Group therapy (counseling) is now widely practiced and has accumulated its own array of more or less well-established concepts and methods. Moreover, group counseling has proved to have certain unique advantages in addition to efficiency. These advantages arise from the opportunities the group method presents for capitalizing on the group-dynamics phenomena that emerge only in collective settings as well as from the prospects for using the aggregate as a vehicle for building the solidarity of groups whose members (as in a work organization) have interdependent responsibilities outside the group.

A different approach to essentially the same problem of time has the most proficient and highly trained professionals cast in quasi-consultative roles. They function as both resource persons and as supervisor-coordinators, informing and guiding the activities of integrated clinical teams that may include lower-level professionals, so-called paraprofessionals, certain laymen, and even patients themselves. These teams depend for success on their cohesiveness and communicative facility and assume at least a modicum of power-sharing by top professionals with other team members. They rely heavily on delegations of responsibility in the interest of furthering the working of the system. The top dog simply has to let go of functions and prerogatives that may once have been defined as exclusively his and content himself with a more general kind of supervisory style than may have been his habit.

Still another clinical innovation has been a reorientation toward what it is that is really the essential object of practice—a changed orientation that concentrates on what is problematic about a person's *behavior*, rather than on what is going on inside his head, and that seeks more efficient problem-solving methods. This orientation is one of the major axioms around which this book is organized. I shall defer further discussion of the behavior-modification school of thought, which has given impetus to this reconceptualization; right now let's look at managerial analogies of the other two modern practices.

The Group Approach

Probably no one has stressed the importance of group methods of management more than Rensis Likert of the University of Michigan. Likert's position makes the group approach more than an expedient to enhance supervisory efficiency. Teamed with a motivational model of managerial control, he regards it as fundamental to effective management. Furthermore, Likert's emphasis on what he terms "the principle of supportive relationships" furthers practices not unlike those of the integrated clinical teams described above. High performance goals are basic to this refrain, but that theme is in counterpoint to others that express preferences for participative decision-making and group methods of management. Some of the flavor of group supervisory practices can be gained from the following extended excerpts from Chapter 4 of Likert's 1967 book, *The Human Organization*:*

> The exact process of these group sessions varies appreciably from unit to unit but is likely to be about as follows: The salesmen meet regularly in group meetings. The number of men varies depending upon the number in the territory but usually does not exceed 12 or 15. They meet at regular intervals every two weeks or every month. As a rule, the sales manager or one of his sales supervisors

---

The Human Organization by R. Likert. Copyright 1967 by McGraw-Hill Book Company. Used by permission of McGraw-Hill Book Company.

presides. Each salesman, in turn, presents to the group a report of his activity for the period since the last meeting of the group. He describes such things as the number and kinds of prospects he has obtained, the calls he has made, the nature of the sales presentations he has used, the closings he has attempted, the number of sales achieved, and the volume and quality of his total sales. The other men in the group analyze the salesman's efforts, methods, and results. Suggestions from their experience are offered. The outcome is a valuable coaching session. For example, if sales results can be improved through better prospecting, this is made clear, and the steps and methods to achieve this improvement are spelled out. After this analysis by the group, each man, with the advice and assistance of the group, sets goals for himself concerning the work he will do, the procedures he will use, and the results he intends to achieve before the next meeting of the group.

The manager or supervisor acts as chairman of the group, but aside from occasional discussions of complex, technical matters, the analyses and interactions are among the men. The chairman keeps the orientation of the group on a helpful, constructive, problem-solving basis. He sees that the tone is supportive, not ego-deflating. He encourages the group to set high performance goals which will help each man realize his full potential.

These group meetings are effective when the manager (or supervisor) does a competent job of presiding over the interactions among the men. Appreciably poorer results are achieved whenever the manager, himself, analyzes each man's performance and results and sets goals for him. Such man-to-man interactions in the meetings, dominated by the manager, do not create group loyalty and have a far less favorable impact upon the salesman's motivation than do group interaction and decision meetings. Moreover, in the man-to-man interaction little use is made of the sales knowledge and skills of the group.

The use of group methods of supervision does not mean that there is no place for leadership. The superior plays at least as crucial a leadership role as he does in any other system of management. The leader has many essential tasks in a System 4 organization. He sees that all members of the group are well trained in group decision making and in group interaction processes as well as in the technical aspects of their work. He seeks through

both group and individual supervision to help each salesman set high and realistic goals for himself and strive
to reach them. He is an important source of technical
knowledge, is responsible for seeing that the unit is efficiently organized and that planning, scheduling, and related activities are done well. He sees that the principle
of supportive relationship is applied. He links the unit
to the rest of the enterprise. He is a source of restless
dissatisfaction with present accomplishments and a stimulus to innovation.

Implicit in Likert's exposition is an extension of his own concept
of the supervisor as a "linking pin" connecting work groups in an
integrated managerial mosaic. In the group itself, the supervisor-coun-
selor-leader has a critical linking role to play. A group, to warrant
the name, must be more than an aggregate of individuals working
in parallel. The contributions to the group process associated with
individuals (and the impediments, too) must be recognized, interrelated, and cumulated. A group-centered supervisor must therefore
strive to discern relations between discrete inputs to the group's
activities, encourage the group to sharpen these perceptions, and
sustain purposeful direction. Indeed, if the supervisor performs his
linking role poorly or not at all, the affirmative virtues of group
supervisory methods risk loss. Then group meetings degenerate into
gripe sessions, conversation rituals, or elaborate coffee breaks. In the
process, the supervisor suffers diminished status.

Most of the specific techniques of group supervision have been
around for a long time—at least as long as the human-relations-in-in-
dustry movement, and that dates from the late '20s. What is newer
perhaps is the idea of including group methods among the building
blocks of managerial systems, rather than merely adding them on
as inessential decorative management flourishes. From the standpoint
of our model individual manager, what is problematic about this
supervisory "new look" is how to infuse familiar standards of group
practice with the counseling perspective and its related skills.

Methods

Procedurally, multiple counseling is more or less but not completely continuous with individual efforts. On the one hand, the
supervisor will find that most of those methods that stand him in

good stead in one-to-one relations will also do so in group settings. To be truly effective in one-to-several relations, however, the supervisor will do well to become more conversant with general principles of leadership and group processes. That extends the scope of knowledge required of the modern supervisor, but it really doesn't overtax it. Good places to begin one's education in these areas might be E. P. Hollander's *Leaders, Groups, and Influence* (1964) and Fred Fiedler's *A Theory of Leadership Effectiveness* (1967).

I do not wish to leave the impression that individual supervision is classifiable with the Edsel or the Spruce Goose; it is now and doubtless will remain fundamental to effective management. But group supervision and group counseling are essential complements to individual methods. Indeed, it seems unlikely that counseling perspectives can ever be successfully inserted into the routine performance of supervisory roles without relating them to more efficient group forms of expression. Moreover, in certain respects, group counseling can be thought of as a kind of coordinate supervision—that is, contributing to a subordinate's individual decisions by skillful use of the facilitating potential of others who share a common fate with him.

Behavior versus Attitudes as Counseling Targets

There is an apparently sensible and therefore resilient belief among experts and men-in-the-street alike that people do what they do mostly because of their individual attitudes, beliefs, and personalities. There are a few souls, though, who suggest that attitudes more or less follow after behavior—that people develop their attitudes in order to explain to themselves and others why they do the things they do, and that what they do is controlled not by what they say but by something quite different.

Now human behavior is obviously a complicated and abstruse subject, the truth of which probably is not available. I shall not get into it any further except to point out again, as I did earlier, that there is at least reason to believe that one may be able to solve problems and accomplish meaningful changes in behavior without plumbing the depths of people's psyches. In other words, to hold a problem-centered focus instead of a personality-centered one does not necessarily condemn one permanently to vistas of trivia.

The Matter of Behavior Change

Among the keystones of counseling described in Chapter 5, I mentioned "listening with understanding." There is no question about the importance of that notion. But if one's concern is ultimately with solving problems and controlling performance (as it must be for managers), then understanding, while necessary, may still not be sufficient to achieving those objectives. On that subject, listen to this section of John D. Krumboltz's book *Revolution in Counseling: Implications of Behavioral Science.**

> *Understanding—Necessary but Not Sufficient.* An alternative notion for conceptualizing a client's problems is to conceive of behavior as already present in the client, waiting to be released by a suitably warm, permissive, nonjudgmental counselor. It is as if good behavior has already been bottled up and needs merely to be uncorked. Under this conception of human behavior each person already knows how to behave, and once he comes in contact with a warm empathic counselor who understands his feelings, then the desirable behavior will be released. Most of us who have taken courses in counseling are very familiar with this point of view.
>
> I must make my position perfectly clear. I do not disagree with the importance of a counselor's understanding. On the contrary, it is essential that the counselor understand the client's problems. Of course he must be empathic and warm. Of course he must hold the client in high regard. Of course he must make it clear that he understands how the client feels. I agree that these conditions are necessary. How else can the counselor find out what is really bothering his client? How else can the client gain that sense of confidence and trust so necessary for an effective working relationship? But I disagree that these conditions are sufficient. More is needed. After the client's problem is clarified and the feelings about it are understood by both client and counselor, the client must still learn how to resolve his difficulty. Understanding alone is not enough. It provides only the beginning step

*From J. D. Krumboltz (Ed.), *Revolution in Counseling.* Copyright 1966 by Houghton Mifflin Company. Reprinted by permission.

upon which appropriate learning experiences can be arranged.

The essentials of positions such as Krumboltz's come down to a pair of precepts especially congenial to my own stated preferences for a problem-focused, job-linked view of the purposes of employee counseling: (1) in particular cases, counseling goals should be expressed in terms of specific behavior changes; (2) operationally, counseling should generally be oriented to direct modification of behavior in its natural setting. Compliance with these precepts demands careful assessment of the problem, joint planning, and attentive monitoring of performance. Those are not such overwhelming tasks as they might seem at first; there are effective procedures available, and there now is ample evidence that one neither has to be a professional to use them nor has to undergo lengthy training to acquire their procedural essentials. Teachers and housewives do it, and so can work supervisors. But before I say more about behavior-modification concepts I should set the stage by mentioning a more customary mode of operation—the nondirective approach to counseling.

NONDIRECTIVE COUNSELING

Most management textbooks, if they discuss counseling at all, feature nondirective ways of doing it. This approach, introduced by the psychologist Carl R. Rogers, was intended by him to contrast sharply with the so-called depth therapies associated with Sigmund Freud and psychoanalysis. Nondirective methods avoid both attempts at diagnosing clients and efforts at uncovering all the deep and presumably unconscious origins of conduct. Instead, the nondirective counselor strives to help the client toward self-understanding by encouraging him to talk about himself and his feelings. The counselor avoids passing judgments or giving advice, yet he conveys an interest in understanding the individual and responds to the client chiefly by trying to reflect and clarify the feelings expressed.

To illustrate the nondirective method: a supervisor might respond to an angry employee who is venting his spleen over having been denied a salary increase with some such statement as: "You feel I haven't treated you fairly" or "You feel I haven't recognized your value to us," instead of simply saying: "We don't have the money and that's that!" (The reader interested in a fuller treatment of nondirective counseling methods in work settings should consult N. R. F. Maier's exemplary *Psychology in Industry,* 1965.)

The nondirective practice of reflecting feelings often feels awkward and pointless to many at first. Yet its nonevaluative character, its prescriptions about not poking around in people's personalities, and its deceptive appearance of simplicity apparently combine to render it easily the most popular model for "how to do it" in the literature on employee counseling. In fact, the nondirective style does have great utility in work environments because it is usually preferable to directive advice-giving.

One might, of course, justifiably wonder why, when a supervisor has good advice to give and knows it, he should refrain from passing it on to the lucky recipient. Obviously, if a situation is as simple as all that, it would be idiotic to sit around reflecting feelings. However, there are three general rules to follow when giving advice: (1) try to make sure you know what you're talking about; (2) don't give advice unless you're prepared to assume responsibility for what happens if it is taken; (3) don't be surprised or hurt if the advisee refrains from taking your advice or even advises you about what to do with it.

Nondirective procedures are certainly useful as general tools for building relationships. But the point is that there are other tactics, better for many purposes, that effective managers can include in their repertoire of interpersonal supervisory skills. With that observation, we can return to a consideration of behavior-modification methodologies.

METHODS OF BEHAVIOR MODIFICATION

These various methods all share an emphasis on specifying behavioral-change targets to be accomplished. They give virtually exclusive procedural attention to behavior *per se* and to achieving change in the natural or normal performance setting. All of them assume a joint mode of action. The employee participates meaningfully in deciding what is to be changed, in planning how it is to be done, and in deciding how the plan will be evaluated. (Others, such as managers, consultants, or union officials, may also participate in the planning process, of course.) In their particulars, these behavior-change methodologies may vary, ranging from comparatively simple stratagems to more complicated programs. Let's take a simple one first.

Behavior contracts. Growing in use, with variations in many settings including schools, an interesting technique that requires little special training involves literally drafting a contractual agreement in which each party commits himself to perform in certain specified ways for some designated period of time. There may be several parties to such contracts—an employee, his immediate supervisor, a higher-level manager—and each signs the agreement.

To illustrate: a worker whose performance is judged submarginal requests a wage increase, which, following negotiation, is set at some specific dollar amount. After obtaining agreement (in writing) by other organizational management whose assent may be necessary, a contract can be prepared. The contract should specify, first, precisely what it is the worker must do behaviorally to obtain any increment in wage. Second, it should specify, after mutual agreement, exactly how the targeted performance changes are to be measured (or indexed) and how and when they are to be monitored. Finally, the behavior or performance contract should spell out what considerations (such as wages) the worker will receive in return for performance changes and should make explicit just how payoff (reward) will relate to performance (behavior change). For instance, in the case cited, since initial performance was submarginal, it might be stipulated that increased payoffs begin only after achievement of some agreed-upon standard of minimum acceptable performance. From that point on, fractional payoff increments could be dispensed in ratio to magnitudes of performance improvement, but perhaps only on condition that performance at an achieved level (or a higher one) be maintained for some minimum time interval. Provision for reducing wage rates in the event of performance degradation could be included in the contract. In any case, it will ordinarily be best if the pattern of payoff in relation to performance is set to yield progressively larger fractions of the agreed-upon total as behavior changes approximate more and more closely the final target performance level. In other words, the payoffs should get greater as one gets nearer the performance target. It is also desirable that the worker and the contract monitor (supervisor) meet frequently to chart progress. Regular meaningful feedback is crucial to the success of the contract or any other behavior-modification technique.

Krumboltz has pointed out that the beauty of the behavior-contract system is that desired behavior is clearly defined. Also, the relation of performance to payoff (called the reinforcement contingencies) are made known ahead of time to all concerned, and the person gets full credit for his changed performance. Of course, attractive as it might be, there will be instances when this technique is unsuitable; union agreements, for example, make the sort of wage-performance contract sketched above infeasible in many situations. Nevertheless, it can be a useful method for many applications that imagination could reveal. And just the disciplining effect of trying to agree on a contract's terms can often help to clarify supervisory missions and issues.

Behavioral engineering. A rather more sophisticated approach to performance control and modification, one that requires at least some special training, is behavioral engineering. Describable in the abstract as the "application of the laws of behavior to practical problems," behavioral engineering amounts to "arranging the environment so that one gets the behavior one wants." Operationally, behavioral engineering is a blend of two technologies: contingency management and stimulus control.

Contingency management is the regulation of what events are contingent on what behaviors. In the jargon of learning psychologists, contingency management is equivalent to the management of reinforcers (loosely, rewards and punishments). Specifying that a worker will receive $2.50 per hour for filing office correspondence is an example of crude contingency management. In other words, the regular receipt by the worker of $2.50 per hour is made contingent on performance of the filing task. Most basic employment contracts exemplify contingency management; bonus and incentive schemes are somewhat more sophisticated and explicit forms of it. What makes it contingency *management* is the formula according to which reward (or punishment) is related to work performance.

Stimulus control is the other component technology of behavioral engineering. It involves arranging events to control behavior or, put differently, bringing behavior under the control of manipulable stimuli. For instance, instructing a hospital patient to press a button when he feels pain exemplifies stimulus control. The pain is the stimulus that is established via the verbal instruction as the controlling condition for pressing the call button. Pressing the button, of course, is rewarded and encouraged by the appearance of a nurse and perhaps by ministrations that lead to lessened pain; that reintroduces contingency management. Stimulus control is also illustrated when a stock clerk is provided with instructions for reordering merchandise in quantities that depend on the number of units of an item remaining on inventory after filling an order. In this case, contingency management is represented by the wage agreement under which the clerk is working.

Procedurally, the fundamental responsibility of the behavioral engineer is task analysis; he must determine (a) exactly what behavior (performance) he wants, (b) what stimuli (signals and events) are to control it, and (c) what reinforcers (rewards) are available to him. He then must put that analysis to work in formulating, sometimes on a trial-and-error basis, a package that can be applied to management problems in the real world.

It should be evident that a particular behavioral engineering package might not operate "on" the individual employee. It might consist entirely of environmental manipulations designed to control the particulars of performance and could be as uncomplicated as a simple physical rearrangement of a work space. Obviously, the well-established disciplines of systems analysis and operations research can therefore be extremely useful in designing engineering packages, as can the newer and possibly more exotic ideas about personal space (see Sommer, 1969). However, it would be a serious error (committed too often in the past) to leave the worker out of the design package unless he is to be eliminated as a factor altogether (via automation, perhaps). In the first place, the engineering package needs to be attentive to so-called human factors (reaction times, dexterity requirements, and whatnot). In the second place, motivation to implement predesigned work systems cannot just be taken for granted. What separates the ideas about behavioral engineering offered here from classical scientific management, therefore, is the pivotal principle that the worker must participate in selecting engineering targets and in planning ways of gaining them and of measuring those gains.

My friend and colleague Tony Graziano points out in a book currently in press that most performance-modification situations are characterized by some combination of two elements: behavior deficits and behavior surpluses. Behavior deficits, as the term implies, are deficiencies or missing components of performance. A first-line supervisor, for instance, might be highly capable technically but weak in handling administrative aspects of his job; that weakness is a behavior deficit. Consider another familiar example: a clerk posting figures commits very few errors but performs at a rate substantially below the norm established for the task; that slowness is a behavior deficit.

Behavior surpluses, on the other hand, are extraneous or unwanted features of behavior. The illustrative hypothetical supervisor might be having difficulty with getting his administrative chores done because he refuses to delegate technical responsibilities. Such refusals point to an area of behavior surplus. The same would be true if, for example, the supervisor made it a matter of high principle to resist the imposition of what he regarded as bureaucratic nonsense. (Assuming, of course, that in fact it is not bureaucratic nonsense.) And in the case of the slow-but-accurate clerk, the fact that slowness resulted from frequent lengthy conversations with coworkers might lead one to regard those conversations as behavior surpluses.

Behavior deficits are corrected within a behavioral-engineering framework by the systematic application of rewards first to successive approximations of and finally to the actual targeted performance. Deficits, in short, are strengthened by a process of shaping behavior, as B. F. Skinner called it, through the use of positive reinforcement (I called it the counseling keystone "accentuating the positive").

The manager interested in using this method will find it helpful to keep in mind the many varieties of reward available for use. Money is not the only one or even necessarily the best one. Indeed, as I mentioned before, simple supervisory approval (compliments, recognition, encouragement) can many times be a potent reinforcer, and it is one readily at hand and controllable by the individual supervisor. Skillful use of behavioral engineering will also be facilitated by explicit recognition of something I have repeatedly advertised in this book: people are not all alike; to be optimal, supervision needs to be individualized. Not everybody finds the same things equally rewarding. The same person may find the same thing differently rewarding at different times. Fortunately, behavioral-engineering methods are adaptable to these constraints.

Whereas behavior deficits are dealt with by using rewards, behavior surpluses are handled by using aversive control (essentially punishment) to weaken them or inhibit their occurrence. We know from our earlier discussion of punishment that the use of aversive control is a tricky business. It requires careful modulation and sound judgment. Many times no actual punishment need be applied. In fact, this is likely to be the most general case in work settings. The surplus behavior can be genuinely weakened simply by ignoring it when it occurs or at least not encouraging it. This is what psychologists call extinguishing a response. It often helps to tell people in advance that you are not going to attend to something they do, but then you must stick to it. If you wish to encourage greater initiative by a subordinate, you might advise him that requests for guidance will be consistently ignored. Such a practice does not preclude either delimitation of areas in which initiative is expected or review of performance in the areas specified. When literal aversive control (criticism, docking pay) is used, it should ideally be done in the interest of preventing the punished behavior from inhibiting the elimination of behavior deficits—that is, the learning of new ways of working. And that view assumes the existence of a development plan for the individual employee.

Thus behavioral engineering is conceptually simple. Despite the abstruse technical jargon that has grown up around it, it consists of basically familiar operations by which people have for a long time gone about getting other people to do things. As in the example about the hospital patient, the difference lies largely in their programmed use and in better understanding of the effects certain operations have on behavior. Often the process is as simple as giving instructions. Unfortunately, that is by no means always true, as anyone will have learned who has ever attempted to devise a productivity-oriented compensation system. Behavioral engineering does require training.

The training required does not, however, have to be either long or arduous. There are basically only two things a good contingency manager has to know and do: (1) identify and reinforce the behavior he wants, and (2) recognize and reinforce approximations to this behavior. Surely these and the other auxiliary skills of behavioral engineering are acquirable by work supervisors.

An Ethical Diversion

The idea of behavioral engineering—indeed, of behavioral control in general—is easy to get into an argument about. It calls forth images of the mechanization of man and the technocratic big brotherism of *1984* and *Brave New World:* modern man no more than a mindless, soulless automaton, bent to the will of a hidden light-flashing, buzzer-sounding, button-pushing, computer-programming elite devoid of any save crassly technical values.

The picture is not a pretty one, and it's not a funny one either, not even in a macabre way. It might have been when it couldn't be done—when the technology was no more than speculation. But now the technology is real, although still primitive, and it can be done. Thus the ethics need to be aired. We cannot pretend as teachers or managers or citizens to operate in some value-free moral void. In particular, whether such technologies as behavioral engineering can be squared with the humanistic-participative view of enterprise management I have stressed in this volume must be faced as an issue.

Without minimizing the importance or the intricacy of the issue, I obviously believe the two can be squared. In essence, this whole book is a brief for a way of doing that—a brief for a way of assuring a managerial posture or context that will guarantee the primacy of human social values and a status for technology as the servant, not the master, of man.

References

Fiedler, F. *A theory of leadership effectiveness.* New York: McGraw-Hill, 1967.

Graziano, A. M. *Programmed therapy: The development of group behavioral approaches to severely disturbed children.* Elmsford, New York: Pergamon Press, in press.

Hollander, E. P. *Leaders, groups, and influence.* New York: Oxford University Press, 1964.

Krumboltz, J. D. (Ed.) *Revolution in counseling.* Boston: Houghton Mifflin, 1966.

Likert, R. *The human organization.* New York: McGraw-Hill, 1967.

Maier, N. R. F. *Psychology in industry.* (3rd ed.) Boston: Houghton Mifflin, 1965.

Sommer, R. *Personal space: The behavioral basis of design.* Englewood Cliffs, N. J.: Prentice-Hall, 1969.

Recommended Readings

Fordyce, J. K., & Weil, R. *Managing with people.* Reading, Mass.: Addison-Wesley, 1971. (Contains a useful presentation of group-management methods.)

Haberstroh, C. J. Organization design and systems analysis. In J. G. March (Ed.), *Handbook of organizations.* Chicago: Rand McNally, 1965. (A sophisticated version of modern scientific management.)

Maier, N. R. F. *Psychology in industry.* (3rd ed.) Boston: Houghton Mifflin, 1965. (Includes discussions of group problem solving by one of the major contributors to research in that field.)

Skinner, B. F. *Beyond freedom and dignity.* New York: Alfred A. Knopf, 1971. (A major discussion of radical behaviorism and its human ramifications by the most articulate spokesman for the viewpoint that behavior is always under the control of environmental contingencies.)

chapter nine

Conclusions
and Caveats

One characteristic of the modern era that I have gone out of my way to stress in this book is what I perceive to be a mounting concern and interest in democratizing authority systems, improving the quality of life within our institutional structures, and meshing organizations more meaningfully with vital human interests. In work organizations, reconciling this cultural thrust with notions of efficiency and productivity has been a central dilemma for theorists as well as for practitioners of management. Moreover, it has been a continuing bone of contention in management-labor relations. Put bluntly, the question is whether an effective work organization can really be concerned with people at the same time that it is concerned with production.

The consensus answer, both theoretically and practically, seems to be a qualified yes. Indeed, any inherent incompatibility of the two concerns now is commonly denied; instead, an essential reciprocity is asserted. In the new management literature, an effective organization is often considered to be one that maximizes task and social-emotional (people) functions simultaneously. And in the paper mentioned earlier, Irving Bluestone (1972) of the U.A.W. commented that there is no inherent reason why increased productivity cannot accompany humanization of the workplace. The problems obstructing accomplishment of this objective have not been overlooked (Chris Argyris reminds us of them regularly—see his *Integrating the Individual and the Organization*, 1964), but contemporary systems-oriented analyses such as I have offered here have sought solutions to these problems by using motivational rather than authoritarian conceptions of organizational control and coordination and by redefining the nature and functions of organizational structures and roles. The operational prescriptions I have noted for enlarged, employee-centered conceptualizations of the functions and responsibilities of work supervisors are almost corollaries to these basic theoretical propositions. As a result of those prescriptions, the modern manager is required to develop high levels of interpersonal as well as technical sensitivity and skill. Sophistication in human needs and group processes, along with skill at transforming understanding into productive supervisory practices, is a firmly established managerial prerequisite. Indeed, in one survey I found that about two-thirds of the respondents rated "ability to understand people" as more important in a work supervisor than technical skill. Finding means for upgrading the interpersonal skills of managers and supervisors must consequently be a high-priority interest in progressive organizations. Sensitivity training, communication-arts seminars, grid training, and other kindred efforts are all aimed at this upgrading, as is the growing endorsement of personal counseling as an acceptable, even essential, function of work supervisors.

However, the unplanned, haphazard introduction of nondescript quasi-clinical practices into the supervisory relationship is likely to be more optimistic than realistic and more fruitless than fruitful. Such practices are also apt to lead to unforeseen consequences subversive of the goals set for the organization. Recognizing that no serious approximation of professional counseling could be part of any rational conception of supervisory functions, I have concluded herein that, for practical purposes, the important thing is cultivation among work supervisors of counseling *perspectives* and *values* as they pertain to supervisory tasks. What I have tried to show is (1) that there is no inherent conflict between the basic concepts of counseling and supervision and (2) that the general principles of counseling applied to the supervisory role can in fact facilitate execution of the essential interpersonal functions of management. My fundamental belief is that organizational productivity and the health and happiness of an organization's members can benefit from improved understanding of managerial perspectives and the acquisition of suitable skills for their implementation.

Precisely what counseling is, as we have seen, can be a subject of some discussion. In one sense, it is an *event*—an encounter between a supervisor and subordinate. In a different sense, it is an *outcome*—the fruition of exchanges arising from creation of a certain kind of supervisory-subordinate relationship. In yet another sense, it is a *process*—the help-oriented application within a participative framework of interpersonal skills that sets loose processes of organizational change, resulting in both individual and system growth. Counseling is, of course, all of these things; and I have urged that it become an *experience* as well—that is, the routine consequence of exposure to supervision by organization members.

To that end, I have pressed the notion that the critical managerial dimension is to be found in the *relationship* between supervisor and subordinate. It is in these relations and the varied exchanges manifest in them that the crucial organizational events take place. Most important of all, perhaps, is the information flow, upward and downward, that makes possible the purposeful operation of organizational systems. Communication is the lifeblood of organizational control, and its effectiveness, in the end, depends less on sophisticated electronic information systems than it does on the building of facilitative human relationships. As a basic aid to achieving and conducting such relationships, I have presented a concept of counseling that is practicable in work settings because it roots its attention in organizational essentials—that is, in tangible relations, behavior, and problem-solving, not in the things going on inside people's heads. I have insisted that counseling must be a line, not a staff, responsibility and have tried to show how it can be. Without retracting that general proposition, certain final cautionary comments are called for.

Like any other set of managerial prescriptions, the counseling perspective makes certain assumptions about the settings into which it is to be introduced and about the people who work in them. Most of these assumptions have been stated one way or another in earlier chapters, but one in particular deserves some further attention. I can state it simply: as an approach to management relying on participative-democratic principles and motivational methods, the counseling perspective depends on organization members having a basic institutional attachment. People needn't be enthralled by their work or passionately devoted to the company, but they must have some minimum commitment—a basic motivation to work and to seek for convergences between the organization's and their own interests.

More often than most of us would like to think, this assumption is perhaps incapable of satisfaction. Whether caused by the meaninglessness of many jobs, or their individual and collective social histories, large segments of society are alienated from work and from our institutional system as a whole. Furthermore, numbers of workers appear to work strictly for extrinsic reasons. They expect to take their satisfactions from life elsewhere than on the job. Counseling, with its associated managerial expectations and baggage, may ask more than they are prepared to give; it can actually constitute an aversive condition that can stimulate interest in finding another, less intrusive job. The medicine, in other words, may sometimes make the illness worse.

The reality of these musings is testified to by the frequent unfortunate fate of job-enrichment programs: they seek reductions in worker alienation but fail to acknowledge the existence of individual differences or of variations in job characteristics. Furthermore, in a small but significant recent book, Walter Neff (1968) has described a not easily produced "work personality" that, like physical capabilities, is fundamental to a person's willingness and ability to work. Like John Kenneth Galbraith, Neff has gone as far as to suggest that, for many workers, trading work for leisure would be a far more attractive prospect than having some portion of the regular work day set aside for group-decision sessions. One might simply choose to delegate to his union the responsibility for guaranteeing to him no worse than minimally acceptable conditions for work and then take no further interest in either the particular job or organization.

It remains to be seen whether, as Perrow (1972) suggests, most organizations will persist in technological forms that are inhospitable to democratic management: "neither so routine as to permit full automation, nor so nonroutine as to permit the decentralization of ends and democracy" (p. 175). But in any event, such a melancholy prospect need not be taken to foreclose aspirations toward more humane and democratic management methods. More than one kind of prophecy can be self-fulfilling. At minimum, we can strive to arrange for widened participation in negotiating the basic terms of the employment contract, if not in all operational details. The question of whether such participation is direct or via representative forms (unions, for example) has a certain ideological significance, but it is not very important practically (provided, naturally, that union affairs are themselves democratic in character).

We must, however, reconcile ourselves to the fact that, since one cannot compel a basic organizational attachment or motivation to work (for one thing, some jobs and organizations don't warrant it and, for another thing, it would be inconsistent with a humanistic, motivational philosophy), the counseling perspective cannot be a managerial panacea. It can undoubtedly help with some of the difficulties hinted at here (such as by reducing alienation from work on the part of some, if not all, workers), but there are management problems that counseling cannot solve by itself. But then neither can any other approach.

The virtue of the counseling perspective is that it does not require adherence to a fixed set of motivational beliefs or management practices nor demand commitment to the myth that there is some "one best way" of managing. By urging a problem-solving stance for managers and a flexible conceptual framework for viewing managerial tasks and by putting people and their diversity at the center of everything, counseling provides a comforting general philosophy of management that retains concrete performance implications and still permits wide latitude for humane individual and situational adaptations. But most important of all is its axiomatic belief that everybody should get as much satisfaction from his work as can be had—what's the point if there isn't at least a little fun in it for everybody?

References

Argyris, C. *Integrating the individual and the organization.* New York: John Wiley & Sons, 1964.

Bluestone, I. Democratizing the work place. Detroit: United Auto Workers, mimeo, June 22, 1972.

Neff, W. S. *Work and human behavior.* New York: Atherton, 1968.

Perrow, C. *Complex organizations: A critical essay.* Glenview, Ill.: Scott, Foresman, 1972.

Recommended Readings

Blauner, R. *Alienation and freedom.* Chicago: University of Chicago Press, 1964. (The standard modern reference on the subject.)

Selznick, P. *Law, society and industrial justice.* New York: Russell Sage Foundation, 1969. (A searching discussion of the "master-servant relationship in industry" and contemporary trends in public and private enterprise.)

Wolfbein, S. *Work in American society.* Glenview, Ill.: Scott, Foresman, 1971. (Looks critically at the properties of the work force, the work environment, and at economic/manpower programs and policies.)

index

179